INTERTHINKING

Through using spoken language, people are able to think creatively and productively together. This ability to 'interthink' is an important product of our evolutionary history that is just as important for our survival today. Many kinds of work activity depend on the success of groups or teams in finding joint solutions to problems. Creative achievement is rarely the product of solitary endeavour, but of people working within a collective enterprise.

Written in an accessible and jargon-free style, *Interthinking: Putting talk to work* explores the growing body of work on how people think creatively and productively together. Challenging purely individualistic accounts of human evolution and cognition, its internationally acclaimed authors provide analyses of real-life examples of collective thinking in everyday settings including workplaces, schools, rehearsal spaces and online environments.

The authors use sociocultural psychology to explain the processes involved in interthinking, to explore its creative power, but also to understand why collective thinking isn't always productive or successful. With this knowledge we can maximize the constructive benefits of our ability to interthink, and understand the best ways in which we can help young people to develop, nurture and value that capability.

This book will be of great interest to academic researchers, postgraduates and undergraduates on education and psychology courses and to practising teachers. It will also appeal to anyone with an interest in language, creativity and the role of psychology in everyday life.

Karen Littleton is Professor of Psychology in Education at The Open University, where she currently directs the Centre for Research in Education and Educational Technology. In 2010 she became Editor of Routledge's *Psychology in Education* book series.

Neil Mercer is Professor of Education and Chair of the Psychology and Education Group at the University of Cambridge, having previously been Professor of Language and Communications at The Open University. In 2011 he became Vice-President of the Cambridge college Hughes Hall.

INTERTHINKING

Putting talk to work

Karen Littleton and Neil Mercer

Routledge
Taylor & Francis Group

LONDON AND NEW YORK

First published 2013
by Routledge
2 Park Square, Milton Park, Abingdon, Oxon OX14 4RN

Simultaneously published in the USA and Canada
by Routledge
711 Third Avenue, New York, NY 10017

Routledge is an imprint of the Taylor & Francis Group, an informa business

British Library Cataloguing in Publication Data
A catalogue record for this book is available from the British Library

Library of Congress Cataloging in Publication Data
A catalog record for this book has been requested

ISBN: 978-0-415-67552-9 (hbk)
ISBN: 978-0-415-67553-6 (pbk)
ISBN: 978-0-203-80943-3 (ebk)

Typeset in Bembo
by RefineCatch Limited, Bungay, Suffolk

Printed and bound in Great Britain by
TJ International Ltd, Padstow, Cornwall

CONTENTS

LIST OF FIGURES

LIST OF TABLES

PREFACE

In any area of research, ideas develop through collective as well as individual efforts.

This book has emerged in part from the 'interthinking' and collaborative work of a number of researchers who have, over 20 or so years, been committed to finding theoretically informed ways of helping people to think together. Special thanks are due to Lyn Dawes, whose creative and inspiring (inter)thinking contributed to the development of the concept of 'interthinking' and who provided constructively critical comments on earlier drafts of the manuscript. The ideas presented here have also been shaped by the work of: Douglas Barnes, Caroline Coffin, Liz Dobson, Derek Edwards, Rebecca Ferguson, Rosie Flewitt, Julia Gillen, Sara Hennessy, Christine Howe, Cindy Kerawalla, Ruth Kershner, Judith Kleine Staarman, Dorothy Miell, Sylvia Rojas-Drummond, Phil Scott, Benson Soong, Alison Twiner, Eva Vass, Paul Warwick, Denise Whitelock, David Whitebread and Rupert Wegerif.

Our thanks go to the Economic and Social Research Council for the financial support provided for some of the research described in this book, and to all those who have participated in our projects. (In order to maintain confidentiality, in the transcribed extracts the names of all participants have been changed.) Thanks are also due to David Shaw who proofread the final version and Bruce Roberts and his team at Routledge for their encouragement and professional support during the writing and production process.

Table 3.1 is reprinted with permission from Dorothy Miell and Karen Littleton; Figure 4.1 is reprinted with permission from Routledge;

Figure 4.2 is reprinted with permission from Routledge and Figure 4.4 is reprinted with permission from Rebecca Ferguson.

Notes on transcription

For our own data we have used a very simple transcription format, in which speech is rendered as grammatical phrases and sentences, to represent the sense that we, as researchers with access to the raw data, made of what was said. Information about equipment, non-verbal aspects of communication and any other contextual information that we considered pertinent to the analysis is to be found in italics in a column or in parentheses. Our judgement was that the inclusion of additional information at our disposal, such as length of pauses or other prosodic and contextual details, would be distracting to readers and irrelevant to the issues we are addressing. Non-word utterances such as 'mm'/'ooh' are included when they are judged to have a communicative function (e.g. to show surprise, agreement, or to extend a speaker's turn in the face of possible interruptions). Words spoken emphatically are in italics. Simultaneous speech is shown by the use of brackets ([ ) preceding each utterance. Where the accurate transcription of a word is in doubt, it is in parentheses. When utterances could not be heard or deciphered, we say so.

1

UNDERSTANDING INTERTHINKING

Introduction

Imagine you are back in school, in a science lesson. The teacher begins the lesson by saying that it will be about the solar system. She says she is going to ask a member of the class to explain to everyone why the moon seems to change shape, over the course of a month. She is looking directly at you. How do you feel? If you are/were a confident and knowledgeable science student, you may not feel at all worried, knowing that you can provide a clear answer. But it is at least as likely that you feel anxious and very unsure that you can provide the right answer. Imagine now a different classroom scenario. The teacher introduces the same topic, but this time she says she is going to give you all five minutes to talk together in groups of three to decide why you think the moon changes shape. One of you will then act as spokesperson for the group, to give the class your agreed answer. Does this scenario make you feel any different? If the prospect of providing an answer now makes you feel less anxious, then that is a tribute to the power of the process we are going to describe in this book – *interthinking*.

Our aim is to explain how, mainly by using spoken language, people are able to think creatively and productively together. We call this process 'interthinking' to emphasize that people do not use talk only to inter*act*, they inter*think*. As we will explain, we consider this ability to be one of the defining characteristics of our species, an important product of our evolutionary history that is at least as important today as it ever was. Many kinds of workplace activity depend on the success of groups or teams finding solutions to problems that arise. Surveys commonly report that an ability to work effectively in teams is one of the characteristics that employers most hope to find in young people joining their workforces. Being able to work with others is also a requirement for active participation in democracy and the life of any community. Although there is a tendency to associate great achievements with the efforts of individuals, recent studies of creative achievement highlight the importance of the intellectual relationships and collective enterprises that those individuals were involved in (see, for example, Sawyer 2012). Interthinking has been necessary for the development and dissemination of all human knowledge and understanding. However, as we will all know from personal experience, collective thinking is not always productive or successful. Two heads are not always better than one, and we need to understand how and why that is the case.

In our earlier publications, we have argued that schools need to help children become more adept at collaborative thinking and problem solving (for example, Mercer & Littleton 2007). Yet this is not widely recognized as an important educational imperative: we have struggled to get government ministers to see that this is as important as the development of children's literacy and numeracy (though teachers more readily understand and recognize that this is the case). In this book, we will justify our stance by explaining how people can learn to use talk to think creatively together and productively, across a range of situations, partly with the aim of persuading more people of the strength of this educational argument. We will consider how the process of interthinking takes place in educational and non-educational settings. One of us has written about such matters before (Mercer 2000), but quite a lot of interthinking by us and our colleagues has happened since then. Using the resources provided by research and examples from various kinds of collective activity, we will explain how interthinking works – why it sometimes goes right and why it sometimes goes wrong. Our hope is that the conclusions we reach will suggest some practical guidance for anyone concerned with maximizing the effectiveness of group-based problem-solving and other creative activity.

Individual and collective thinking

We are both psychologists, and as students we found that learning and problem-solving were treated in psychology as processes that individuals engage in alone. At the time, that seemed quite reasonable; but it seems less sensible now. In our experience since then – as psychological researchers, colleagues at work, carers of young children, teachers and learners and in life more generally – learning and problem-solving have commonly been social, and highly communicative, processes. Faced with a problem, people do not usually depend only on what they each have stored in their individual brains.

In everyday settings, as opposed to in psychological laboratories, people rarely tackle problems in strict isolation. They depend a lot on each other to find out what they need to know, and commonly work with others to create new knowledge and understanding. Even in schools, where we have done most of our research, and where the products of individual learning are regularly assessed, it is hard to separate the process of 'learning' (by which is generally meant the acquisition of some new knowledge or skill by an individual) from 'teaching' (meaning the active efforts of another person to help them gain new understanding). Learning is improved by good teaching, and good teachers achieve the best results with attentive, highly motivated learners. In everyday life, solving problems commonly involves interactions with other people and it is usually motivated by shared concerns and goals. Success in achieving shared goals depends, in part, on how well people communicate with each other while pursuing them, so understanding how to maximize the effectiveness of interthinking could be of real practical value. However, the ubiquity and importance of thinking collectively has not been reflected in the extent or scope of research about it. The study of the process of interthinking, and of the role of language in it, has been strangely neglected.

Reading the works of other researchers in psychology, linguistics, sociology and other relevant subjects, we have often felt that we were going to turn the next page and find that interthinking would be analysed and explained. This includes such influential, engaging and informative books as *Creative Collaborations* (John-Steiner 2000), *Group Creativity: innovation through collaboration* (Paulus & Nijstad 2003), *The Stuff of Thought: language as a window into human nature* (Pinker 2007), *Why We Collaborate* (Tomasello 2009) and *Language: the cultural tool* (Everett 2012). Instead, however, we would turn the pages to find authors setting off on a different trajectory, pursuing an answer to their own (perfectly legitimate) line of enquiry. Taking the route we expected them to take would no doubt have seemed to them a diversion from their intended journey. But we have still found their work useful. To differing extents, those publications, and others we will refer to throughout the book, all reflect a growing recognition of the way that language, in both its form and use, is thoroughly integrated with the cognitive processes humans use to make sense of the world and to solve the problems they jointly encounter.

The fields of research on which we will draw are quite disparate: they include applied social psychology, developmental psychology, the sociology of organizations, neuroscience, linguistics, philosophy and educational research. As we will go on to describe in Chapter 2, there have been some important studies by applied social psychologists of team-based activity in the workplace. There has also been a good deal of research on collaborative creativity (as discussed in Chapters 3 and 5) and on collaborative learning and problem-solving in educational settings (which we will refer to in Chapters 4 and 5). Educational researchers have mainly been interested in how collaborative learning helps improve the understanding and attainment of individual students, but such research also helps us understand the processes by which people learn and interthink successfully together. There is a wealth of research in developmental psychology and linguistics on how children's early use of language, through their involvement in dialogues with older people, helps their cognitive development. In Chapter 5 we will draw some conclusions from its findings about how people learn to successfully 'co-regulate' their joint thinking activities.

Our evolution as interthinkers

The study of human evolution has been, for most of its history, the province of biologists; but in relatively recent years it has also been actively colonized by psychologists and social anthropologists. One of their main interests has been in understanding the development of the human brain, not so much as a physical structure but as a distinctive, indeed unique, functioning organ. They have therefore aimed to explain how evolutionary pressures on our ancestors in the battle for survival could selectively favour some kinds of thinking capability rather than others. Initially, this tended to focus on individual intelligence, with claims that those individuals who could process environmental information most effectively would be able to grasp chances for survival that others less able would not. In line with the biologist Richard Dawkins' (1976) influential book *The Selfish Gene*, these accounts tended to focus on individual sensory and information-processing abilities and how competition between individuals who were better or worse endowed in that respect resulted in them having more or less offspring. That is, it was argued that as a species we evolved with increasingly complex brains because of competition among humans, and not only because of the competitive struggle with members of other species.

More recently, it has been suggested by some evolutionary scholars, such as Robin Dunbar (1998), that an explanation of our evolutionary success that relies only on the ability of individuals to process environmental information is not well matched to the capacities of the human brain. Instead, it has been suggested that the design and capacity of the human brain reflect the survival advantages of being able to make sense of complex social relationships. Becoming able to organize communities in which people took on a variety of complementary roles gave early humans a survival advantage over other species, but it also created new cognitive demands on individuals. Evolutionary psychologists thus became interested in a topic that had been studied hitherto by social psychologists: 'social cognition', which means how people notice and respond to the subtle social signals of those they are interacting with, even if they are not consciously aware of doing so. It has been known for some time that when people interact, they tend to 'mirror' each other's gestures and postures (e.g. Chartrand & Bargh 1999). There has been much curiosity among evolutionary scholars in the discovery by neuroscientists of 'mirror neurons' in the brains of primates – including humans – which 'fire' when an individual observes a community member carrying out an action that would involve those same neurons if the action were carried out by the observer (Mukamel, Ekstrom, Kaplan, Iacoboni & Fried 2010). It is rather as though the observer acts out a mental version of the activity they observe. However, this 'mirroring' apparently only happens when *intentional* actions are observed, suggesting that it is linked to interpreting what someone else is doing. Commenting on this, the neuroscientists Frith and Singer (2008: 3875) say: 'Through the automatic activation of mirror systems when observing the movements of others, we tend to become aligned with them in terms of goals and actions.'

It is now quite widely accepted, then, that in our evolutionary past, the survival of our ancestors was dependent not only on their individual ability to make sense of experience and to coordinate their actions with those of others, but also to empathize with the mental states and intentions of their companions. That is, they became able to imagine what the world might look and feel like from someone else's point of view. This empathic capability is called 'theory of mind' (Premack & Woodruff 1978). As the psychologist Grist (2009: 44) explains:

> We become aware of others because our brains can apply 'theory of mind' – this is the cognitive endeavor of attributing thoughts to others. Part of theory of mind consists in thinking about what other people are thinking about other people – 'what does Jane think about Tom's behavior towards Pablo, given that Pablo is upset about his father's illness?' This is a very complicated kind of cognition and is, as far as we know, unique to humans.

This would all seem to integrate well with our own perspective on the importance of collective thinking – that survival is assisted if members of a group or community can combine their individual brains into a collective problem-solving tool and so jointly overcome the challenges their community faced through sharing relevant knowledge and reasoning together. However, this is not, typically, the direction that evolutionary psychologists, anthropologists and neuroscientists have taken in their accounts of human thinking. Rather, they have argued that a well-developed capacity for understanding social relations and inferring another person's cognition and affect is valuable because it will assist an *individual's* success in competition and combat (e.g. Harcourt 1988, cited in Dunbar *op. cit.*). Taking a similar individualistic perspective on evolution, the linguistic philosophers Mercier and Sperber (2011) argue that the human capacity for reasoning should primarily be understood as a competitive social mechanism, rather than a collaborative one, because the main survival aim for each of us is to persuade others to do what we want. They suggest that this would enable the offspring of those individuals most effective at reasoning to outnumber those weaker at reasoning in future generations, though it is not clear why. It seems to us that the more obvious function of argumentation as a collective activity among our early ancestors is that it would enable a group of people to identify the best of several possible courses of action, so that they would have a better chance of surviving as a group. This function, however, is not considered relevant by Mercier and Sperber because it does not fit the dominant individualistic account of the mechanisms of human evolution.

It seems, therefore, that a growing recognition of the inherently social nature of human cognition – the basis for what is now often called 'the social brain hypothesis' (Dunbar *op. cit.*) – is merely being used to generate a new level of individualistic explanations for why some of our individual ancestors managed to survive in their world better than others, and how some people today are able to negotiate and manipulate the social world to their own advantage. Indeed, alternative accounts of human evolution that argue for the importance of cooperation and altruism, as proposed by the sociobiologist Edward Wilson (2012), have been fiercely attacked by Dawkins and other evolutionary scholars (see for example, Dawkins 2012).

We do not feel competent to reconcile feuds among evolutionary scholars, but surely any account of human evolution needs to explain why we developed one of the most distinctive of our capabilities, which is that we are able to engage collectively in reflective, creative, goal-orientated, knowledge-building activities. Competition between individuals may well provide part of the explanation for the evolutionary origins and nature of human cognition; but accounts based only upon this fail to acknowledge one of the most important characteristics of our species: we solve problems by interthinking and reasoning collectively. In any case, do accounts of human evolution have to be either individualistic *or* collective? As Wilson (*op. cit.*) argues, explanations of differential survival can be pitched at the level of the community, as well as the individual. As an emergent species, our ancestors would have an advantage over competing species because they became able to use language and other modes of representation to define common problems and goals, and plan how to deal with them in advance. Moreover, those communities that had members who were able to think well together might be expected to have an advantage over other communities in which individuals pursued their own courses of action. We suggest that the crucial evolutionary step in human development was when a community of individuals became able to achieve better solutions to some of life's problems than any individuals could on their own. The research on team-based activity in the workplace that we will present in Chapter 2 supports this view that, under some conditions, two or more heads are definitely better than one.

Language and interthinking

Our account of interthinking gives language, and particularly spoken language, a central role. This does not mean that we are unaware that other modes of communicating, for example using pictures and non-verbal actions, can enable people to pursue the achievement of greater understanding together. Rather, it reflects our belief that language is the most important mode for enabling us to think collectively. As we will explain, there has been some relevant research by linguists that has revealed how different genres of language have been designed to suit the kinds of joint tasks that people engage in. Surprisingly, not much attention has yet been given to understanding how language functions as an interthinking tool. Social psychologists acknowledge the vital role language plays in social encounters, and we will draw on their research in several ways; but they do not often treat the analysis of talk as the analysis of the process of thinking collectively. While there is, as we acknowledged earlier, a major field of social psychology called 'social cognition' (see, for example, Fiedler & Bless 2001), it is concerned with the sense people make of social encounters (for example, through their interpretation of the subtle signals of speech or body language) rather than how language is used for collective, creative problem-solving. Within social anthropology, linguistics and linguistic philosophy, there has been much research on how language is used in social settings and how it can be used to represent ideas. However, the role of language in the dynamic process of thinking collectively has seemed to fall outside the domains of those subjects too. Nevertheless, research in all those fields mentioned above is potentially very useful for pursuing our interests here. We hope to show that a focus on language as a tool for thinking collectively can bring together, for the first time, some interesting ideas from very different areas of research.

The cognitive psychologist Steven Pinker has claimed that 'simply by making noises with our mouths we can reliably cause precise new combinations of ideas to arise in each other's minds' (1994: 15). At one level, this may seem an uncontroversial claim: people use talk to share information with each other all the time. But on closer examination, this claim is patently false, as anyone knows who has suffered the embarrassment of discovering later that they seriously misunderstood the meaning of what someone had said to them, although it seemed quite straightforward at the time. While we all use language to share information, often effectively and with some precision, it cannot be described only as a means for safely transmitting ideas in a precise, unchanged form from one individual brain to another. Any characterization of language use that implies a linear process in which people initially form their ideas and then share them, thus exchanging the results of their separate, individual intellectual efforts, is a misrepresentation. That characterization is wrong because it neglects the crucial significance of the dynamic interplay and interaction of minds in conversation, and the cultural and social context in which any conversation takes place. 'How are you?' means something different if it is addressed to you by your doctor at the beginning of consultation, an evangelist calling at your door or by a friend who knows you have just been through a gruelling job interview. 'I'm having an old friend for dinner' carries a special meaning for members of an audience when spoken by Hannibal Lecter in *The Silence of the Lambs*. The meaning of any combination of words can vary, depending on what knowledge resources a listener brings to making sense of them. However, this does not reflect a weakness of language as a means for enabling collective thinking, it represents one of its creative strengths.

Language's power as a 'cultural tool' for pursuing creative, collective thinking partly lies in the possibility that listeners may each interpret a speaker's words in rather different ways, depending upon the personal perspective and background knowledge they bring to the conversation. The Russian literary scholar Bakhtin (1981), writing early in the twentieth century, proposed that we do not make sense of what someone says to us simply by matching the words spoken to definitions in a mental dictionary. Rather, we use any of our available knowledge that we judge as relevant to make sense of them, and in that process generate our response to what has been said (even if we do not speak it aloud). Any one person's interpretation of what someone else has said, or written, will be affected by the relevant knowledge they bring to bear. In an extended conversation, the common knowledge you are building with your conversational partner through your shared history can help you derive deeper meanings from what they say than the superficial meaning of their words would suggest. The resources of relevant knowledge available to any listener or reader for making sense of language can change over time. University scholars throughout the world still feel it is worthwhile trying to determine the meaning and significance of the words of philosophers, poets and other creative thinkers (such as Bakhtin), which were spoken or written, often quite clearly, a long time ago, because they can bring new ideas into play for making sense of those original words.

Nevertheless, it might seem that the collective process of creating under-standing would be better if language operated reliably for making meaning, in the way that Pinker describes. But is that really so? If effective language use was simply a matter of making meaning unambiguous, why should anyone value, say, the lyrics of the songs of Bob Dylan when it is often unclear what they are about? Would Shakespeare's plays be better if each character's lines had been designed to transmit one, unambiguous meaning (if that were possible)? As a cultural tool, language offers much more interesting possibilities *because* it is not always reliable for causing precise meanings to be generated in someone else's mind. Rather, what one person says acts as a catalyst for activating the thoughts of a listener. In a conversation an attentive listener draws on whatever knowledge they have that seems relevant to making sense of what has been said, and also so that they can contribute to the continuing, joint process of sense-making. This is one way that new knowledge is created. In using language to make joint sense of their experience, two people may create a new kind of understanding that neither could have achieved alone – which they may both then go on to express in words for the consideration of others.

We are not arguing that all thinking is collective, or even that all creative thinking is collective; but thinking collectively is such a common and natural part of human life that we are surprised that so little has been explained about how it works. Nor would we ever suggest that language underpins all thinking, collective or individual. We are convinced, however, that language enables some of the most powerful interthinking to be done. Any collaborative learning and problem-solving must necessarily involve the joint management of a task; and language is most commonly used as the medium of management in such situations. Working effectively as a group involves using language to create knowledge and co-regulate activities. Language can be shaped into special varieties to serve this purpose. The technical discourses of crafts and professions – their specialized genres – which we will discuss in Chapter 2, are not only efficient ways of representing technical information, they also often embody the ways of thinking that are used by members of any particular community of discourse. This is why the linguist Martin (1993) has described genres as not merely varieties of language, but as rule-governed, goal-orientated social processes embodied in language. In relation to our interests here, they enable the thoughts and actions of individual members of the relevant communities to be aligned and coordinated.

The relationship between individual and collective thinking

Unlike all the other animals with whom they were competing for survival, our pre-historic ancestors became able to use language to organize, review and plan their collective activities. Importantly, they also became able to use it to induct the members of each new generation into their complex society – which is in part why and how the institutionalized practices of education originated. What is more, language is both the medium and the message; we learn our first language through using it. It provides us with ways of representing experience and for reasoning, collectively and alone. Language links cooperative activity with individual cognition: on the one hand, people are able to think collectively; and on the other, such collective activities impact upon the development and process of individuals' thinking. The Russian psychologist Vygotsky, a contemporary of Bakhtin in the early-twentieth century, was one of the first to offer a theory of cognitive development that recognized the role language played in that process (Vygotsky 1962, 1978). As he put it, the development of children's thinking is shaped by the dynamic relationship between *intermental* activity (social interaction) and *intramental* activity (individual thinking), with language as the prime mediator between the two. We suggest that it is not just the development of cognition that depends on that relationship; the distinctive nature of human thinking in general is instantiated in our ability to think both collectively and alone, and for these two modes of thinking to operate in complement.

To explain the relationship between individual and collective thinking, something more than an individualistic theory of cognition and learning is obviously required. Some existing concepts can be useful for constructing such an explanation. One is 'theory of mind', which we introduced earlier. Two others are 'metacognition' and 'co-regulation'.

'Theory of mind' capabilities do not only allow us to assess others' emotional states or try to exert a social influence on them; they also enable us to assess what 'common knowledge' we share with another person, and judge their levels of understanding or skill in relation to ours, and regarding particular topics or tasks. Common knowledge is a dynamic, accumulating resource, which participants in a conversation both generate and rely upon to communicate (Edwards & Mercer 1987/2012; Jeong & Chi 2007).

In ways that are not possible for other species, humans can use language to take account of the relative states of knowledge and understanding of participants, and proceed accordingly, in educational and other spheres of activity. Both theory of mind (assessing what others think and know) and metacognition (reflective awareness of our own thought processes) are involved. They allow us to jointly instigate the practical cycles of planning, acting, reflecting and re-planning by which we solve problems, share knowledge and construct new joint understandings.

A third useful concept is 'co-regulation', which we will consider in more detail in Chapters 4 and 5. It has emerged from research on how young children learn to plan and manage their activities in social settings (Volet, Summers & Thurman 2009, see also Mercer & Littleton 2007), but there is no reason why it should only be applied to children's activities. Vygotsky proposed that children's intermental experiences of being regulated by adults provide a model for the intramental regulation of their own individual behaviour. Similarly, the ways their social behaviour is regulated by adults can help children learn how to regulate their own collective behaviour, when they are working in a group. This is very apparent in the kinds of play activities children become involved in when left unsupervised; there is commonly order of a kind, not chaos. The shift from external regulation to internal regulation is often represented in the games themselves. A popular game for five- to eight-year-olds is 'school', whereby one of them takes on the regulating role of the teacher and others act out the roles of pupils (often naughty ones: see Elbers 1994). As they get older, children exercise their collective creativity by inventing new games and new rules with which to play them. In these ways, children learn how to take on (from their adult carers) a responsibility for controlling, monitoring and reflectively assessing their collective behaviour. As we will see in later chapters, the effectiveness with which adults are able to co-regulate their interthinking activities can affect the quality of the outcomes of their efforts.

Understanding and explaining interthinking

As mentioned earlier, psychological theories and accounts of learning and problem-solving have traditionally been focused on individual thinking, and have given little attention to how we do those things collectively. We need an explanatory framework for bringing together, in a coherent way, concepts that will help us to understand interthinking. It needs to be able to take account of the cultural and social basis of human thinking, and of the use of language as both a means for communicating socially (a cultural tool) and for thinking individually (a cognitive tool). There is a suitable candidate for such an explanatory framework, *sociocultural theory*, which has been built from the legacy of Vygotsky's work. Many of the claims he made about the relationship between culture, social interaction, language and children's cognitive development remained unsubstantiated by hard evidence until research based upon his ideas began to be pursued in the latter part of the twentieth century. As we have explained in our previous book (Mercer & Littleton 2007), evidence has now been found that supports the socio-cultural kind of explanation of the development of thinking that Vygotsky first offered.

Sociocultural theory is also known more grandly as *cultural-historical activity theory* (CHAT), and this lack of a single name reflects the fact that it is does not exist in any single, authoritative form (as explained by Daniels 2001, 2008). Moreover, it has mainly been designed as an explanation of cognitive development and learning, not to explain the ways people use language to creatively seek solutions to problems together. What we require for our purposes here is a sociocultural account of collective thinking in general, and one of our intentions is that this book provides at least a preliminary sketch for this. We will offer the results of our efforts in Chapter 5.

Analyzing talk as collective thinking

The methodology we use to understand how people use talk to think together is called *sociocultural discourse analysis* (SCDA), and some of the other researchers whose work we draw on in the book have used the same, or a similar, approach. Along with our colleagues, we have developed SCDA over the last 20 or so years, in the course of research that has been reported quite extensively (see, for example, Mercer 2004; Mercer, Littleton & Wegerif 2004; Mercer and Littleton 2007). However, we cannot assume that readers of this book will have read our earlier publications. Therefore, to make the analysis clear and accessible, we will summarize here the ideas we think are most relevant and important for analyzing talk as collective thinking, and explain a little of their history. This is not a book on research methodology, so we will not go into much detail about analytic methods, in this or any of the subsequent chapters. Any readers wishing to know more will find relevant publications and resources on our Thinking Together website (http://thinkingtogether.educ.cam.ac.uk).

The term 'discourse analysis' can be used to refer to several different approaches to analyzing language (both spoken and written) and to quite different methods. Within linguistics, its use typically indicates an interest in the organization and functions of language in use, and can be applied to research on monologic, written texts as well as dialogue. Within sociology, psychology, anthropology and educational research, it usually refers to the analysis of talk in social context. In sociology 'discourse' can also be used to refer to the general social climate of ideas associated with a topic rather than specific conversations and so some discourse analysis may constitute a branch of cultural studies. However, while the analytic approach we use has been informed by the work of language researchers in several disciplines, it possesses its own distinctive characteristics.

In our analysis of talk, we are interested in how it is used as a social mode of thinking – language as a tool for teaching-and-learning, constructing knowledge, creating ideas, sharing understanding and tackling problems collaboratively. Given this focus on talk as a form of intellectual activity, SCDA differs from 'linguistic' discourse analysis in being less concerned with the organizational structure of language and more with its content, how it functions for the pursuit of joint intellectual activity and the ways in which shared understanding is developed, in social context, over time. Like some linguistic analyses, SCDA may focus on the lexical content and the cohesive structure of talk, especially across the contributions of individual speakers, because word choices and cohesive patterning can represent ways that knowledge is being jointly constructed. A sensitivity to the way talk happens within institutional and cultural contexts is central to SCDA, as is any information we can gather about the knowledge that participants might be bringing to bear on what they say and do. For this reason, it differs from the approach to analyzing talk called 'conversation analysis' (as exemplified by the work of Drew and Heritage 1992; see also Schegloff 1997) because knowledge that is not explicitly invoked by speakers, and the social and cultural context of their talk, are considered legitimate concerns. Moreover, as our sociocultural analysis is concerned not only with the *processes* of joint cognitive engagement but also with their developmental and learning *outcomes*, it differs from analyses rooted in discursive psychology (cf. for example, Edwards & Potter 1992), which are only concerned with communication processes. As in linguistic ethnography and conversation analysis, reports of the analysis are typically exemplified by selected extracts of transcribed talk, to which the analyst provides a commentary. However, it is also important to note that SCDA can involve the complementary use of both *qualitative* and *quantitative* methods of analyzing talk (as first discussed in Wegerif and Mercer 1997). By qualitative analysis we mean the careful examination of particular episodes of interaction among members of a group engaged in a particular task, in order to understand how they are both invoking and creating knowledge and understanding. By quantitative analysis we mean using computer-based methods to examine the way certain aspects of talk, such as the frequency of use of certain words, changes over time. In some of our research we have also used quantitative statistical methods to assess the learning gains or problem-solving outcomes of groups of children working together, and related these to our analyses of their talk; but we will not be drawing those findings to any great extent in this book.

The combined use of qualitative and quantitative analyses of talk enables us to combine a detailed analysis of talk in specific events with a comparative analysis of dialogue across a representative sample of cases. For this latter kind of analysis, we have to deal fairly easily and quickly with quite a large language corpus (such as one consisting of many hours of transcribed conversation). To do so, we have combined qualitative, interpretative methods with the use of computer-based methods developed for text analysis in the field of corpus linguistics. Concordance software enables any text file to be scanned easily for all instances of particular target words. Commonly used examples are Monoconc, Wordsmith and Conc 1.71. Recent versions of qualitative data analysis packages such as NVivo also offer some similar facilities. We include an example of that kind of analysis in Chapter 4, and refer to other findings from it in Chapter 5. In the years since it emerged from the research that we will describe in the next section, SCDA has enabled us to characterize and explore the nature of classroom talk and its educational significance in a range of settings.

The nature of talk in groups: three types of talk

Back in the 1980s, one of us (NM) was fortunate enough to be involved in one of the first research projects to study how children talked together in primary school when they were asked to work in pairs or groups at the computer (see Wegerif and Scrimshaw 1997). It was called SLANT, Spoken Language and New Technology. Those were the first days of this 'new technology' in classrooms, and it was as much due to the scarcity of machines as to a wish to promote group work that teachers began to sit children in groups to carry out computer-based activities related to science, mathematics, history and other subjects. This was also an era in which, as is the case when we are writing this book, the educational policy of the British government had taken a 'back to basics' turn, which involved describing group work as a waste of time and asserting the need for a return to the formal didactics of the traditional classroom. Members of our team were not convinced by the government's rhetoric, and one of our hopes was that through observing, describing and analyzing children's talk in groups, we would be able to show that such collaborative activity was beneficial to their learning.

Imagine our dismay back then when, after watching and analyzing many hours of recordings of children talking and working together, we had to admit that a lot of it was, from an educational point of view, probably a waste of time. We saw children going off task, ignoring each other, shouting each other down, working in parallel rather than together and arguing in a confrontational, unproductive way. Sometimes we would see groups behaving more cooperatively, sharing relevant information and interacting in a friendly manner – but still not really tackling problems collaboratively or thoughtfully. This was all rather depressing, and it seemed that we would have to become government supporters rather than critics, on this educational issue at least. But then, among the wealth of observational data, some very reassuring discoveries started to appear. We identified evidence of some groups of children doing what could only be described as 'thinking together'. They all took part in sharing information, reasoning about it and staying well on task. Members of these groups seemed to trust each other enough to feel they could be critical about each other's ideas without falling out, and they tried hard to reach some kind of consensus. It also seemed that these groups were best at finding and devising good solutions to their problems, and that it was likely that the individuals involved would leave the group having learned something useful about the topic in question. The problem remained, however, that these gems of collaborative activity were rare in the data, and so a concern that group work was often not productive was justified. The conclusion we drew reminded us of the words of one of the nursery rhymes we had heard some young children chanting in school: when group work in the classroom is good, it is very, very good; but when it is bad it is horrid. We set out to describe the variety of talk we observed with more precision, identify the kinds of conditions that generated it and to think of ways that the incidence of the most productive kind of talk could be maximized. As this book shows, we (and several of our colleagues) are still engaged in this task.

After many hours of video analysis and discussion, members of the SLANT team finally agreed that we could usefully distinguish between three kinds of talk in groups (as first reported in Dawes, Fisher and Mercer 1992). They are can be summarized as follows.

1. *Disputational talk* in which
    • there is a lot of disagreement and everyone just makes their own decisions;
    • there are few attempts to pool resources, or to offer constructive criticism;
    • there are often a lot of interactions of the 'Yes it is! – No it's not!' kind;
    • the atmosphere is competitive rather than co-operative.

2. *Cumulative talk*, in which
   - everyone simply accepts and agrees with what other people say;
   - children use talk to share knowledge, but they do so in an uncritical way;
   - children repeat and elaborate each other's ideas, but they don't evaluate them carefully.
3. *Exploratory talk*, in which
   - everyone engages critically but constructively with each other's ideas;
   - everyone offers the relevant information they have;
   - everyone's ideas are treated as worthy of consideration;
   - partners ask each other questions and answer them, ask for reasons and give them;
   - members of the group try to reach agreement at each stage before progressing;
   - to an observer of the group, reasoning is 'visible' in the talk.

Most of the talk we had observed resembled the first two types, Disputational and Cumulative, rather than the third – yet the third type was the kind of talk, Exploratory Talk, that we judged to be the most educationally effective. We took its name from the work of one of the classroom talk researchers we most admired, Douglas Barnes, who had observed something like it in his own research on how secondary school students 'thought aloud' in a group when freed of the pressure to present ideas formally to a class (Barnes 1976/1992). However, we elaborated his original account of it to put more emphasis on its interactive features, as in the definition above.

Our team in the UK was not alone in being interested in identifying the most educationally productive forms of talk in groups. Lauren Resnick and colleagues in the US (Resnick 1999; Wolf, Crosson & Resnick 2006) independently identified a kind of discussion that they call 'accountable talk'. Their description of it bears strong similarities to our own definition of Exploratory Talk:

> For classroom talk to promote learning, it must have certain charac-
> teristics that make it *accountable*. Accountable talk seriously responds
> to and further develops what others in the group have said. It puts
> forth and demands knowledge that is accurate and relevant to the
> issue under discussion. Accountable talk uses evidence in ways appro-
> priate to the discipline (for example, proofs in mathematics, data
> from investigations in science, textual details in literature, documen-
> tary sources in history). Finally, it follows established norms of good

reasoning. Accountable talk sharpens students' thinking by reinforcing their ability to use knowledge appropriately. As such, it helps develop the skills and the habits of mind that constitute intelligence-in-practice.

(Resnick 1999: 5)

Exploratory/accountable talk will figure prominently in our discussion of how people think effectively together, but it is important to note that Cumulative Talk can also be useful at certain points in a group's deliberations, as we will illustrate later in the book. However, despite the observed frequency of its occurrence in classrooms, there is little good to be said for Disputational Talk (except perhaps as a way of 'letting off steam' when discussions get too intense).

We can illustrate the kinds of interaction these three types of talk are meant to characterize by some examples from classroom data. Extract 1.1, from the SLANT data, was a classic example of the kind of talk that led the research team to define Disputational Talk. In it, two boys aged 11 years are working at the computer on a puzzle (part of a mathematics software developed by Smile Mathematics) in which they have to determine at what co-ordinates on a grid map of New York an elephant is hiding.

EXTRACT 1.1 Disputational Talk

Lester: I can do it.

Shane: (*Still staring at the screen*) No, not up, down.

Lester: It can't be.

Shane: It can.

Lester: I know where it is. (*Shane takes his turn, but fails to find the elephant*)

Lester: I told you it weren't over there. (*He then takes his turn, without success*)

Shane: Eh heh heh heh. (*Laughing gleefully*)

Lester: Which one just went on? I don't know. (*Apparently talking to himself*)

Shane: 1,2,3,4,5,6. (*Counting squares, also apparently talking to himself*)

Lester: I know where it is.

Shane: I got the nearest.

Lester: (*Counting squares*) 1,2,3,4,5,6,7,8.

Shane: I got the nearest, 5.

Lester: So it has got to be 1,8.

Lester: 2,8.

Shane: Oh, suit yourself.

The two boys talk a lot as they pursue the task, but other than Shane's second comment 'No, not up, down', none of the talk seems to be aimed at achieving a joint goal. Some of the talk is just individual 'thinking out loud' and when they do interact it is mainly to assert a competitive stance.

In Extract 1.2, two ten-year-old girls are trying to write a fictional dialogue together in which one girl tries to bully another girl into giving her some money. The way they build up a stock of shared ideas, pursuing the dialogue without any challenges or explicit reasons, led us to classify it as Cumulative Talk.

EXTRACT 1.2 Cumulative Talk

Sally: Yeah. What if she says erm erm "All right, yeah." No, just put "Yeah all right." No, no.
Emma: (*Laughs*) No. "Well I suppose I could . . . "
Sally: " . . . spare 15p." Yeah?
Emma: Yeah.
Sally: "I suppose . . . "
Emma: "I suppose I could spare 50p."
Sally: "50?"
Emma: Yeah. "Spare 50 pence."
Sally: "50 pence."
Emma: "50 pence." And Angela says "That isn't enough I want to buy something else."
Sally: Yeah, no no. "I want a drink as well you know I want some coke as well."
Emma: "That isn't enough for bubble gum and some coke."
Sally: Yeah, yeah.

Extract 1.3 illustrates the kind of interaction that generated the definition of Exploratory Talk. Three 11-year-old children are doing an activity about the Vikings, using a computer-based activity. In the role of a group of Viking invaders, they are planning a raid on the British coast, and have to use the information available to choose between a limited set of options for how to proceed.

EXTRACT 1.3 Exploratory Talk

Diana: Let's discuss it. Which one shall we go for?
All: (*Inaudible – reading from instructions*)
Peter: 1 2 3 or 4. (*Reading out the number of options available*) Well we've got no other chance of getting more money because
Adrian: And there's a monastery.

Diana: And if we take number 2 there's that (*inaudible*).

Peter: Yeah but because the huts will be guarded.

All: Yeah.

Adrian: And that will probably be guarded.

Diana: It's surrounded by trees.

Peter: Yeah.

Adrian: And there's a rock guarding us there.

Peter: Yes there's some rocks there. So I think I think it should be 1.

Adrian: Because the monastery might be unguarded.

Diana: Yes 1.

Adrian: 1 yeah.

Peter: Yeah but what about 2? That, it might be not guarded. Just because there's huts there it doesn't mean it's not guarded does it? What do you think?

Diana: Yes, it doesn't mean it's not. It doesn't mean to say its *not* guarded does it. It may well be guarded I think we should go for number 1 because I'm pretty sure its not guarded.

Adrian: Yeah.

Peter: Ok, yes, number 1. (*He keys in 1 on keyboard*)

In Extract 1.3 we are witnessing three people interthinking. They share relevant information and reason about it. They question each other's ideas, but in the interests of achieving their joint goal, rather than to assert individual dominance, they ask each other what they think, they all participate and they appear to reach consensual decisions.

The three types of talk are not meant to be categories into which all observed discussion can be neatly assigned. We deliberately picked the three extracts above from the large dataset of more ambiguous examples, just to convey the essential idea of each of the types of talk. Talk is messy stuff, and does not fit neat categorizations (despite the continuing struggles of those researchers who are committed to coding talk into mutually exclusive 'boxes' for their analysis). The typology is rather a heuristic device, a way of 'seeing the wood from the trees' in what would otherwise be a confusing forest of data. The typology could probably be made much more sensitive to functional variations in the talk of working groups if we expanded the numbers of types of talk to match more precisely the kinds of tasks, or stages of a task, groups are involved in, and if it took into account the different roles speakers adopted. However, once one undertakes that kind of development, the categories proliferate indefinitely and the explanatory elegance of a three–part characterization is lost.

Having first found this three-part typology useful for understanding classroom talk, we have since realized that it is also useful for understanding the variety of talk in many non-educational situations. Many readers, we are sure, will have sat through committees, staff meetings or project team meetings in which Disputational Talk was common, with some Cumulative Talk happening now and again, and very little Exploratory Talk to be heard. One can tune in any day to televised sessions of the British parliament to hear a formal, erudite, well-presented and yet highly unproductive version of Disputational Talk taking place, but very little reasoned discussion of an 'Exploratory' kind.

Ground rules for talk

To understand how and why different types of talk are generated in groups, we have to appreciate the ways that social norms shape people's behaviour. Like all social practices, the three types of talk are the products of our 'social brains'. We are able to organize and carry out quite complex social activities because we can establish social norms, or rules, for how we should interact to get specific kinds of things done. A term we have adopted from the discourse of sport to describe these norms is 'ground rules'. The idea of there being 'ground rules for talk' emerged from work with the discursive psychologist Derek Edward (Edwards & Mercer 1987/2012). The ground rules for any kind of event generate its familiar and distinctive patterns of talk, even if participants are not consciously aware that these rules are operating. Lectures, debates, doctor–patient interactions, job interviews and conversations on first dates all will happen as participants expect they will if they all know, and follow, the appropriate ground rules. For example, the usual ground rules for students attending lectures include: do not talk (loudly, at least) while the lecturer is speaking; raise your hand if you want to ask a question; and keep your questions and any other public utterances short and to the point. Within the culture of any society, ground rules exist for all its usual types of social events. But that does not mean that only one possible set of rules can be invoked for any one kind of event, or that the norms that usually apply are necessarily the best ones for achieving the participants' goals. It might improve students' understanding and learning outcomes if the ground rules for lectures were changed, so that students would be expected to take an active role in the event, perhaps by engaging in at least some extended discussion with a lecturer. Any lecturer wishing to make their sessions more interactive would have to engineer a change in the ground rules to make this happen. However, changing the kind of talk that happens in a group activity is often not easy. It requires some explicit recognition of what rules participants are following, and some agreement that different ones should be followed instead. As we will go on to show, making group-based activity creative and productive may require some explicit consideration and revision of the ground rules being applied.

Three levels of analysis

To describe and evaluate the actual talk that goes on in any collaborative activity, we need to incorporate the models of talk into an analysis that operates at three 'levels'. We are using the term level here to mean something analogous to the way 'depth of focus' is used in photography. The first level is *linguistic*: we need to examine the talk as spoken text. What kinds of speech acts do the participants perform; do they assert, challenge, explain or request? What kinds of exchanges take place between them? How do speakers build their conversations; do they respond and react to each other's talk? We can also consider what topics are introduced, and whether they are 'picked up' by some or all members of a group and carried along through the discussion, or whether they sink from the flow of talk like a stone. It is at this level that we can see that Disputational Talk is dominated by assertions and counter-assertions, with few of the repetitions and elaborations that characterize Cumulative Talk. Exploratory Talk, in comparison, typifies talk that combines challenges and requests for clarification with responses that provide explanations and justifications.

The second level is *psychological*: an analysis of the talk as joint thinking and action. How do the ways the speakers interact, the topics they discuss and the issues they raise express their interests and concerns? To what extent is reasoning being pursued visibly and jointly through the talk? We may be able to use the types of talk to typify the kind of communicative relationship that the speakers are acting out. So, for example, in Disputational Talk the relationship is competitive; ideas are asserted rather than shared, differences of opinion are emphasized and not resolved, and the general orientation is competitive and defensive. Cumulative Talk seems to operate more on implicit concerns about maintaining solidarity and trust, rather than seeking the best possible outcomes, and requires the constant repetition and confirmation of partners' ideas and opinions. Exploratory Talk requires that the views of all participants are sought and considered, that proposals are explicitly stated and evaluated, and that explicit agreement precedes any group decisions and actions. Both Cumulative and Exploratory Talk seem to be aimed at the achievement of consensus, while Disputational Talk does not. In Disputational Talk, although a lot of interaction may be going on, the reasoning involved is very individualized and tacit. In

Cumulative Talk, by comparison, ideas and information are certainly shared and joint decisions may be reached; however, there is little in the way of challenge or constructive conflict in the process of constructing knowledge. Exploratory Talk, by incorporating both conflict and the open sharing of ideas, represents the more 'visible' pursuit of rational consensus through conversation.

The third level of analysis is *cultural*. It involves some consideration of the kinds of events in which talk is taking place, and the kinds of ground rules the speakers seem to be following (do these result in everyone participating, and/or in some people exerting more control over the conversation than others?), the institutions in which those events are located and the kinds of reasoning that are valued and encouraged within those cultural institutions. At this level, Exploratory Talk can be described as a cultural tool for reasoning collectively. Its ground rules embody certain principles – of accountability, clarity, constructive criticism and receptiveness to well-justified proposals – which are valued highly in many societies. In many of our key social institutions, for example those concerned with law, government administration, research in the sciences and arts and the negotiation of business, people have to use language to do several things: interrogate the quality of the claims, hypotheses and proposals made by other people; express clearly their own understandings; reach consensual agreement and make joint decisions. One would expect to find Exploratory Talk to be in common use in such settings. However, we all know too that the kind of open, democratic and free debate represented by Exploratory Talk is not always apparent. It may be considered threatening to an established order or prevailing consensus. As we will show later in the book, this may be one reason why group activity is often not as creative or productive as it might be.

Concluding remarks

In this chapter we have argued for the historical and continuing importance of interthinking, and the need to understand it better. We have also argued that understanding the relationship between individual thinking and collective thinking depends on a proper appreciation of the role of language for linking intermental and intramental activity. In making these arguments we are not denying the significance of studying individual thought processes. We have no wish to set individualistic and collective accounts of problem-solving, or of creativity, against each other; but we are arguing for a new balance to be established in research into the processes of human thinking, so that collective thinking processes are accorded the significance they deserve. As we hope to show, this could have some useful, practical outcomes.

2

TALK AND INTERTHINKING AT WORK

Introduction

Our research on the language of collective thinking has mainly been undertaken in schools and other educational institutions. Much of the interest, from teachers and researchers, in students working together in the classroom has been motivated by the desire to know if collaborative learning helps individual learning. We can confirm that it does, though only if the conditions are right (Mercer & Littleton 2007; Howe 2010). But that is not the only good reason why it may be useful to get children to work together, and to help them to do so effectively; skills in solving problems collaboratively will be useful to them in the rest of their lives, and not least in the world of work. In Chapter 1 we argued that the emergence of the ability to interthink is likely to have have played a major role in the evolution of our species. Occupations in which we have to plan and solve problems together are as common today as they have ever been. It is widely recognized that having the ability to work well with others is a very desirable attribute in an employee – the advertisements for jobs as varied as accounting assistant, coffee shop manager, IT salesperson and university researcher commonly say something along the lines of 'candidates should be good at working in a team and possess excellent interpersonal skills'. In this chapter, we will review research on how adults work together in groups to get things done, in actual work situations and in simulated activities, and discuss what this tells us about the characteristics of effective teamwork and the role of talk in the deliberations and interthinking of a team. We will relate the results of that research to our own analyses of talk among groups of students in school, and draw some conclusions.

Studies of group problem-solving in work environments

In this section, we will consider research mainly carried out by psychologists and sociologists, focused on the success or otherwise of groups engaged in solving problems or completing work tasks. The evidence from such research about what makes groups and teams effective in pursuing joint tasks is variable in nature and quality. Much of it is based on reflective reports of what people said happened, rather than actual recordings of people working together. Other evidence comes from simulated activities, commonly involving complete strangers put together for that purpose by researchers, rather than real-life work colleagues, and so will inevitably lack some aspects of authentic situations that might have important influences on behaviour, such as the team members having a history of working together and occupying different statuses within an organization (as is typical in the world of work). Moreover, the evidence does not lead directly to any simple conclusions. As one team of experienced researchers of team activities has commented: 'We do not know of a study that has clearly demonstrated . . . enhanced performance of teamwork relative to working as individuals' (Paulus, Dzindolet & Kohn 2012: 348). Surprisingly, there seem to have been few detailed studies of how spoken language is used in working groups, least of all those that are seeking creative and effective solutions to problems. Even when authors include illustrative examples of talk, they are rarely the subject of close analysis. We will often have to extrapolate from this available evidence to make connections with our interests here.

The findings of research on the value of collaborative learning in schools are somewhat paradoxical, supporting both the value of group work and pointing to its common failure to be productive (Mercer & Littleton 2007; Howe 2010). The same applies to research on collective activity at work, which shows that groups seem to achieve some of the best, and some of the worst, outcomes. One well-established concept used to explain why groups are often not creative or successful in their thinking is 'groupthink'. Apparently first used by the American journalist William Whyte (1952), the term was taken up by the psychologist Irving Janis (1972, 1982) to explain the tendency of members of well-established, autonomous groups to rely entirely on each other's views and ignore and dissent or criticism from outside their immediate circle. His account of it was not based on experimental studies, but on his case-by-case analysis, using the documentary evidence available about why some grave errors of judgement had been made and carried through at senior level by groups working within the American government – such as the decisions made during the 1960s to invade Cuba and to continue the war in Vietnam, when it seems so much evidence available at the time to decision-makers militated against such actions.

The nature and characteristics of group behaviour in general are not our concern here, but rather how the communication processes within groups help or hinder innovative, productive thinking. Nevertheless, we can learn something about this, indirectly, from Janis's study. He suggested that one reason that groupthink happens is because members of some of the groups he discusses – government ministers and their civil service advisors – were often very similar in background and values. They shared similar values and respected each other's judgments over those of non-group members. They tended to talk with each other (about the relevant issues) to the exclusion of 'outsiders', however well qualified they might be. They wanted to maintain solidarity rather than explore dissent. Because of these factors, when trying to make a decision, they reached a consensus quickly and any evidence that was not in accord with their shared judgements was quickly rejected. The dynamic processes of the group created obstacles to the pursuit of creative, innovative solutions to the problem they were dealing with. In other words, some unspoken 'ground rules' governed the way discussions were being conducted among policy makers, inhibiting certain kinds of speech activities and encouraging others. Among the various characteristics and symptoms of groupthink, Janis included two that he considered particularly important. We can recast them here as ground rules for how members are expected to talk within the kind of malfunctioning group he was describing:

1. Members should not express arguments against any of the group's majority views.
2. Alternative options to the majority views, and sources of support for those options, should not be offered or explored.

Other such rules might include 'do not express any views that might undermine consensus', 'do not question the judgement of a senior colleague', 'provide support rather than criticism' and 'use any opportunities to express support for the official group stance'. These rules reflect social factors such as the relative status of group members, which have to be taken into account in understanding any specific collective's tendency to 'groupthink'– but by considering the problem in terms of implicit ground rules for talk, it becomes easier to see the implications for what could be done to avoid the problems of groupthink.

Hart (1994) carried out an analysis of how groups in American government reach decisions, and Esser (1998) reviewed a series of 17 empirical studies on this phenomenon. Both drew similar conclusions to Janis. Baron

(2005) reviewed evidence from even more recent research, drawing the conclusions that while the occurrence of groupthink does not require the specific antecedent conditions that Janis claimed (such very strong, cohesive relations within a group), it is a much more widespread phenomenon than he suggested. However, some organizational researchers (e.g. Peterson, Owens, Tetlock, Fan & Martorana 1998) have argued that groupthink is not nearly so common a phenomenon as Janis and others have claimed, suggesting that poor decision-making within an organizational team can be explained in more conventional terms, for example by followers' unquestioning deference to a charismatic leader. On balance, though, the evidence supports the view that certain kinds of social conditions encourage groups to make bad decisions.

Our concern here, in any case, is not with the *antecedent conditions* that might be claimed to generate groupthink. It is instead with the ways in which groups deal with tasks in discussions – and so with what are usually called the *symptoms* of groupthink. There is less controversy about these, as Baron says:

> It is not surprising that symptoms of groupthink (e.g. self censorship, rejection of criticism) or the defective decision processes these symptoms are thought to produce (e.g., poor information search, inadequate risk assessment) lead to low-quality decisions. Indeed, it would be remarkable if they did not.
>
> *(Baron 2005: 226)*

There is evidence from experimental psychological research to support Janis' arguments about the tendency for groups to reach uncritical consensus when strong majority views are expressed. For example, in a series of studies, Nemeth and Kwan (1987) found that people asked to provide associations to words (that is, to provide a list of ideas suggested by words) tended to adopt the expressed view of the majority, even if it was not in accord with their initial judgements; and faced with a near consensus, members of groups tended to ignore the potential alternatives. Whether or not one is convinced about the widespread prevalence of groupthink, one might be tempted to conclude that any tasks requiring innovation, or imaginative decisions, would best be attempted alone.

To counter this negative view of group activity, one might turn to Surowiecki's *The Wisdom of Crowds* (2004). This book was not based on any specific empirical study of how people interthink, but is rather an insightful argument by an American financial journalist of why 'groups' or 'crowds' (loosely defined) regularly come up with better solutions to problems than individuals. His ideas are backed up by reported examples from the arts, sciences, politics, business and law. Much of his interest, though, is not with small group activity, but rather with how the average of the very disparate judgements or predictions of a large number of individuals (a 'crowd') commonly provides a more accurate solution than an individual expert (for example, in predicting the vagaries of the stock market), even if they do not share their views. While that is not so relevant here, in one chapter he also reviews what is known about small group activity, about what various studies have suggested make teams or groups work well or badly. He concludes that experimental, laboratory-based studies support the importance of ensuring that communications among partners are as effective as possible, with conditions that are optimal for 'group idea exchange', as Paulus *et al.* (*op. cit.*: 348) put it. Janis's own suggestions for avoiding groupthink are predicated upon the principle of 'vigilant decision-making'. This requires group members to become metacognitively aware of the risk of groupthink occurring, and act accordingly. At least some members have to adopt and maintain a critical stance, perhaps by taking on the role of 'devil's advocate'.

Following Janis's (1982) original suggestions, several researchers, for example Hirt and Markman (1995), have investigated the effects of asking a group member to act as a 'devil's advocate'. This person's role was to identify potential flaws in any proposed solutions or courses of action; this seemed to discourage tendencies towards groups reaching consensus without exploring all the options. However, devil's advocates are often perceived for what they are – someone acting out a role. Nemeth, Rogers and Brown (2001) found that the interventions of such false critics could actually have the effect of bolstering any existing majority point of view. Authentic critics, who genuinely harboured doubts about proposals, were more likely to stimulate the consideration of a wide range of relevant ideas. Nemeth and Kwan (1985) also found that when someone in a group dissented from the majority view, other participants within the group were more likely to offer original ideas of their own. The influential research of Charlan Nemeth and her colleagues on group processes, carried out over several decades, has shown the value of constructive forms of dissent for stimulating productive outcomes and the most creative solutions (see, for example, Nemeth 1995). It seems that groupthink can be avoided by encouraging genuine dissent, as long as that dissent is constructive and aimed at enabling the group achieve the best possible outcomes.

One of the obvious reasons why two (or more) heads can sometimes be better than one is that two or more people represent a larger resource of knowledge, skills and experience than one person. Of course all that potentially useful knowledge is only actually useful if it is shared. On the basis of a meta-review of studies of information sharing, researchers have concluded that:

> Teams typically possess an informational advantage over individuals, enabling diverse personal experiences, cultural viewpoints, areas of specialization, and educational backgrounds to bring forth a rich pool of information on which to base decision alternatives and relevant criteria. However, the current findings confirm that although sharing information is important to team outcomes, teams fail to share information when they most need to do so.
>
> *(Mesmer-Magnus & DeChurch 2009: 544)*

In summary, then, psychological and sociological research on group activity has highlighted several features of group interaction associated with good outcomes, and several that are associated with bad outcomes. We will consider how these features relate to our own analyses of talk in groups, towards the end of the chapter.

Creative talk within, and across, professional boundaries

Solving problems and doing creative work, within any specific field of expertise, are likely to involve the use of special, distinctive vocabulary and ways of using language. This is because such activity rarely starts from scratch; it is more usually a case of building upon the foundations of the shared, existing knowledge of a community of work to reach into the unknown. Within any domain of activity, there is no virtue in re-inventing a wheel; it is better to build on what is already known by wheel experts as the basis for creating a new and even better version. Any discussions about what a better wheel might be like will be more efficient if everyone involved already knows what key terms such as axis, bearing, rim and so on mean. In some subject areas, such as particle physics, efficient discussion will depend on all participants being familiar with an extensive and precise technical language, which is incomprehensible to outsiders. It is only justifiable to call such technical language by the pejorative term 'jargon' when it is used inappropriately, in settings where everyone who needs to understand what is being discussed does not speak that language. Within what can be called a 'community of discourse' (Swales 1990), a technical language allows ideas to be shared, considered and developed rapidly. Apart from its communicative efficiency, its use can also help build solidarity among co-workers, as using technical language signifies membership of a particular profession. Sometimes this latter function becomes more important than communicative efficiency. A striking example is the colourful argot used by Wall Street traders during the 1980s, as described by Kathleen Odean (1990). 'James Bonds' were those that would mature in the year 2007, while shares in Kelloggs were known as 'Cornflakes'. The 'macho' culture of that work environment was reflected in the traders being described as 'jackscrewing' the market, 'killing' orders and 'churning' customers.

Talk is an important tool in collective work, even in occupations that might not normally be associated with language use. Research carried out in Canada and the UK by the linguist Peter Medway (1996a, 1996b, 1996c) focused on the talk between architects and the builders and other skilled workers who had the job of turning the architect's plans into reality. Of course, construction workers had drawings representing the architect's plans to work from; but, as Medway says, 'Speaking, in the sense of performing speech acts such as requesting, asserting, ordering, promising, denying and proposing, is precisely what drawings cannot do' (1996a: 108).

Apparently the best laid plans of even the most accomplished architects encounter problems when they are translated from two to three dimensions. It becomes apparent that a duct will obstruct a view from a window, or that wiring cannot run where intended. Therefore, talk is required, through which a 'virtual building' can be constructed ahead of the real one. For this to happen, all the participants will not only need to share a common conception of their goal, they will also need to have some shared values and – crucially – a shared language for talking about the technical aspects of the job in hand and finding creative solutions to the problems they encounter. Medway describes how the talk on building sites was often a combination of technical discussion aimed at solving problems and banter that reinforced the relationships between workers – as in this extract from a discussion between an architect, Clem, and an architectural technician, Ollie, a younger man working under Clem's authority. They are finalizing the design for a staircase in a house.

EXTRACT 2.1 The staircase

Clem: We'll have plaster walls, with cut strings.
Ollie: With a cut string? What's a cut string?
Clem: Where you see the edge of the treads, to the tread.
Ollie: What, the treads actually coming through the string?
Clem: Yes, come through, an extra eighth, it's a lovely staircase, I haven't drawn one of those for years.
Ollie: The sort of stairs we've got is a return stair.

Clem: Yes. Ooh, I'm beginning to like this. If you do a cut string you can
        be my friend.

(Adapted from Medway 1996c: 5–6)

We see here that, although they clearly share some technical vocabulary,
Clem has to explain the meaning of 'cut string' to his junior colleague. In
the complete sequence from which this extract comes, we can also discern
how the relative status of the participants gives them more or less control
over the direction and outcomes of the talk.

Teaching is a profession strongly associated with the use of talk. In
Chapter 5 we consider some ways that teachers can enable their students
use talk for interthinking – but how can teachers use talk for their own,
professional, learning? In Japan a self-help approach to professional
development called *Jugyou kenkyuu*, usually translated as 'Lesson Study', has
become very popular in recent years – though its origins can apparently
be traced back to the nineteenth century. It typically involves a group
of teaching colleagues (usually between three and six) getting together
to identify an aspect of their teaching that they think will improve their
students' learning. They then spend time working on this together; it seems
that this can be anything from about ten weeks to three years. They watch
each other's lessons, either 'live' or on video and analyze them together. At the
end of the period they may teach a 'public research lesson' before an invited
audience of colleagues from their own and other schools. An introductory
explanation of Lesson Study (in English) can be found in Yoshida (2002)
and on several university websites, and at the time of writing is becoming
popular in the US, in Britain and in several other European countries.
Available evidence suggests it is a very effective method for improving
teaching.

The process of lesson study is, by its nature, very dependent on teachers
talking together and reaching some joint agreement about what works and
what does not in the classroom, and planning what to do about it. We have not
had direct access to any Lesson Study discussions among Japanese teachers,
but Peter Dudley (2013) carried out his doctoral research at Cambridge
on how this practice was taken up by teachers in England. He recorded
Lesson Study discussions among groups of teachers in two primary schools.
One of his interests was in the kind of talk that the teachers engaged in,
and how well this enabled them to explore the pedagogic issues they were
pursuing and plan to respond to them appropriately. One of his findings was
that the most productive sequences often resembled the kind of discussion
that, in Chapter 1, we called Exploratory Talk. The teachers' Lesson Study
discussions critically considered what had happened in the observed lessons,

but did so in a constructive, mutual way. Being teachers, they commonly used technical terms in those discussions to describe each others' observed actions (such as 'closed questions', 'probing questions' or 'guided writing' and so on); interestingly, Dudley found that through their exploratory discussions teachers often realized that they had very different understandings of exactly what some of those terms referred to. He comments:

> Some of the most significant teacher learning that took place was rooted in members' growing awareness and discovery of these differences in interpretation ... They were then challenged by the LS [Lesson Study] process to acknowledge these differences and to renegotiate and align their collective understandings in order to proceed.
>
> *(Dudley 2011: 130)*

We can see two teachers (Lloyd and Yolanda in the transcript) tackling this kind of issue in Extract 2.2. They had been talking about ways of teaching writing, and one of them (L) had just said he proposed to carry out some 'guided work' with his whole class.

EXTRACT 2.2 Guided writing

Yolanda: (*After a long pause – and in amazement*) You're going to '*guide*' the whole class?!

Lloyd: That's what I had in my head from last time.

Yolanda: SSss maybe I'm missing something, but this is not what I conceive to be guided reading ... (*corrects herself*) guided *writing*.

Lloyd: The *shared* writing.

Yolanda: The 'shared' writing I would take as the whole class.

Lloyd: We do it as the whole class but ... we're kind of mixing it with guided writing as well ...

Yolanda: Guided writing is your group.

Lloyd: Guided writing is when the children write something themselves.

Yolanda: (*Simultaneously*) and the focus for your group to take their learning forward and the next step for them.

(Adapted from Dudley op. cit.: 116)

The teachers continued to debate this issue for a while, with Yolanda eventually commenting:

Yolanda: I think we're probably doing the *same things*, but when we say it, we're using different terminology and language.

(Dudley op. cit.: 117)

Within a group of co-workers, who share a community of discourse, interthinking in the context of such joint activity can be greatly assisted by the use of technical language; but even in such discourse communities, assuming a shared understanding of what is meant may sometimes be risky. When the job in hand involves people from different professional or occupational backgrounds collaborating, the use of particular discourses can be even more problematic. It has become common in recent years to extol the virtues of interdisciplinary working, with people from different professional backgrounds (and 'user' backgrounds) being brought together to seek creative solutions to problems. In such interdisciplinary teams, members can offer complementary forms of expertise and share different kinds of relevant experiences. Hearing how a problem is perceived by someone from a different background can also be helpful in revealing how one's own view of issues has been constrained, and sometimes unfortunately, by the typical conditions of working within just one community of expertise or relying only on one kind of knowledge resource. This may enable more creative solutions to be found. However, this kind of interdisciplinary or interprofessional working is not without its challenges, and it depends on participants being able to communicate effectively. Introducing an analysis of such kinds of collaborative activity, the psychologist Anne Edwards offers the following relevant anecdote:

> I recently spent an afternoon walking around villages in rural France with an architect who had been involved in their restoration over several decades. His passion for stonework, sight lines and field systems was compelling ... His expertise came from engagement in practices which were culturally formed with specific histories and values. However, he became anguished when recounting the problems he had with town planners. It was clear that when an architect tries to work with a town planner, what matters for each of them may not easily align, intentions get thwarted and frustrations result.
>
> *(Edwards 2012: 22)*

In the research on inter-professional working that she then goes on to describe, Edwards did not study architects and town planners, but people from different professional backgrounds who were expected to work together to provide what are in the UK called 'children's services', such as social workers, teachers and educational psychologists. Partly in response to some high-profile stories of child neglect, there came a strong directive from the UK government in recent times that such services should be 'joined up' rather than based on a set of separate professional domains, so that children did not slip through gaps between those domains. This created a need for meetings involving professionals from different backgrounds – social workers, teachers, health professionals and police – who had often never worked together before. On the basis of her experience of these meetings and of interviews with these care workers, Edwards argues that one of the most crucial requirements for 'joined up' activity is that all involved establish a firm basis of common knowledge about the issues and cases in question. In other words, there needed to be talk that would create foundations of shared understanding among the various professionals, before they could get down to discussing the cases of the children they were concerned with. The professionals themselves found that they needed to give special attention to how they communicated with each other. One of the directors of children's services interviewed said she had to become 'a story teller, I use metaphors, trying to get people to see things they haven't seen and I use their language to talk about what we are here for' (Edwards *op. cit.*: 30).

Talk in working groups

One of the few studies we are aware of that has analyzed the talk of groups of adults engaged in a creative work task is by Middup, Coughlan and Johnson (2010). They recorded two groups of four people who were working together to produce short video sequences, for use on a university campus, to encourage students and staff to recycle waste. The researchers were interested in mapping the joint creative process involved (through a series of meetings over three weeks), and also in assessing the efficiency and effectiveness of the groups in achieving their goals. Middup *et al.* generated a model of the process, which would represent the track of a group's deliberations and how members used talk and action to move from an initial conception of their goal to the eventual outcome. They suggest that this involves members of a group progressively modifying the 'conceptual space' of their task, so that they may move from a broad and relatively ill-defined notion of what they are about to a narrower, more appropriate and more achievable version.

We can now look at two extracts (or 'vignettes' as the researchers call them) from their recordings of the groups in their study. A, B, C and D are the participants who speak during the vignettes.

> **VIGNETTE 2.1 Taken from Meeting 2 of Group 1**
> The use of sound in the film is discussed, as C is interested in presenting some facts and advice to viewers. B and A are interested in how this may be done, and suggest the possibility of reading the facts out audibly. C then suggests that sound may not always be audible, and

the group adopt the concept that the sound used in the film will only be complementary. C is explaining some of the advice he feels the film should get across.

B: How do you want to do that? I mean do you just want someone reading out these facts or some pictures . . .

C: No I have to admit I haven't worked on that.

A: I would think it could be pictures and then you reading the facts, which relate to the pictures . . .

C: Umm, I'm thinking if that is to be played in the Parade (*a bar*) or in the public streets, maybe sound is not an option.

A: That's true.

C: Or maybe we should have sound only as a complementary channel, and we should have the facts bring it out. So we have a quote displayed. You can have voice on top, but not dependent on it.

A: Yeah true.

C: We can have sketches that are without dialogue, and have some nice music on top, if it's not being played it's not necessary.

(From Middup et al. *2010: 214)*

The researchers comment that 'Vignette 2.1 represents a common pattern for this type of meeting, where ideas that have been formed by an individual prior to the meeting are introduced as concepts to the group, which are then discussed, modified and ultimately either accepted or rejected as the group members collaborate on these aspects of the task' (214). We might also note that this extract has several features of Exploratory Talk: speaker A asks C a question, to obtain some clarification of C's ideas and C responds appropriately; A makes a new suggestion, which is then challenged, with a good reason, by C; and A expresses agreement to C's new suggestions. We do not hear from participant D in this vignette, and B makes only one contribution, but overall the interaction is constructively critical.

The next extract comes from the second meeting of another group, who were involved in a similar task.

VIGNETTE 2.2 Taken from Meeting 1 of Group 2

The group are generating and discussing ideas for their film. The concept that the film is to be a reminder to people to recycle is suggested by A, and elaborated by A and B. A further concept of using animals is suggested, then – due to questioning from C – is elaborated to be animal noises that grab attention by A and B. D then interjects, noting that these noises may be irritating when in a public place.

A: Perhaps the film is just a reminder, I just forget to do it (*recycling*).

B: So you are talking about someone passing by?

A: Talking about someone passing by, I quite like this idea of reminders as you pass by.

B: OK you pass by and you see something, a message, just saying LOOK! This is the recycle bin . . .

A: Well I think the silly animal trick is quite funny sometimes . . .

C: How does that go?

B: Noise?

A: Well you just have an animal

B: Oh I see, you just have an animal . . . it grabs attention.

A: You have that . . . people like animals it grabs attention.

C: So a cow?

A: Ducks . . . 'What's that duck doing there?'

B: OK that's interesting, you hear the sound of an animal, but it has nothing to do with animals. You hear the animal then you look at the screen and . . .

A: It's just a thought, it's a trick, you see it a lot in adverts on the tele (*vision*).

D: Yeah, it's a good idea but if we're putting it somewhere where a lot of people are walking past . . .

A: Is this going to make them fed up.

D: It's going to make them crazy . . .

(From Middup et al. 2010: 217)

The researchers make these comments about Vignette 2.2:

> As the animal and noise concept is ultimately rejected, the progress that seemed to have been made is reversed, however, the actions of the group are not without value – they have aided definition of the group's conception of the outcome, which has now been reduced in scope to disregard ideas that might irritate people through inappropriate use of sounds in a public space. Their conception now does include (and focuses on) possibilities for reminders that grab the attention of passers by, encouraging them to recycle . . .Later the group adopts a modified version of this idea, using film characters rather than animals, which would be less likely to "make them (*passers by*) fed up". This fitted better with their conception of the outcome – reminding people to recycle in a public space – but still contained much of the essence of the ideas presented here.
>
> *(Middup et al. 2010: 217)*

So although the group's 'exploratory' discussion of the animal idea did not immediately provide a solution to the problem, it focused the group's attention on a key aspect of the task in hand – and they drew indirectly on the ideas generated later.

Regarding Vignette 2, they also comment:

> This instance demonstrates how support for creative collaborative tasks must take into consideration the tension between support for *effective* collaborations and support for *efficient* collaborations. In this case, an intervention could have been made to reduce the conceptual space earlier. If this were to be done, then the group's activity would be more efficient as their activities would be slightly more deterministic; however, reducing this space reduces the range of potential solutions, meaning that unless care is taken to understand the space in which effective outcomes exist, the group could be prevented from devising and producing the most effective outcome to their task.
>
> *(Middup op. cit.: 218)*

Middup and colleagues also offer some insightful comments on the kinds of problems that groups working on a creative task can encounter. The narrowing of conceptual space is a necessary part of achieving a solution to a task; but if it is done too early or too readily in a group's deliberations, it may prevent them from considering a wide range of relevant ideas and so lead to less creative outcomes. It might seem *efficient* for the group to move quickly to a narrow, more focused definition of the task and the range of possible outcomes, but that might not, in the end, make their interthinking more *effective*. This tension between efficiency and effectiveness would need to be made explicit in a group's reflective consideration of its own activities. They also suggest that groups commonly encounter problems because members' initial conceptions of the task do not match the task requirements or practical constraints involved in pursuing it. They call this 'concept mismatch'. A third kind of problem, which they call 'artefact mismatch', is when the cultural tools and resources available to a group are at odds with their initial ideas about how to pursue their goal. Avoiding or overcoming these kinds of problem would presumably require a group to introduce a ground rule requiring that task definitions and available resources are expressly considered before the creative work begins. This kind of analysis helps us see more clearly how the success of collective thinking activities depends on the ways discussions are organized and monitored, and how task constraints and the tools available for pursuing tasks need to be taken into account.

Concluding remarks

We have reviewed a range of studies of how people work together, and a common theme has been whether collective activity achieves better creative outcomes than solitary endeavour. As with research on collaborative learning in the classroom, the outcomes of this research seem, on first consideration, paradoxical or even contradictory. On the one hand, there is evidence that collective endeavour can be highly creative and productive; and on the other that it very often is not. This paradox can be resolved, to some extent at least, through the realization that we are not dealing with a single social phenomenon. There are many ways that groups of people come to work together, and they vary in how they are constituted and in the kinds of tasks they engage in. Nevertheless, drawing on our own research and the research we have reviewed in this chapter, we will cautiously offer some general conclusions about the characteristics of discussions most likely to help working people interthink to achieve creative and effective solutions to problems – and avoid the 'groupthink' trap.

To ensure that a group discussion is to be productive, it seems that participants should do the following things:

1. freely express critical views about any proposals made by fellow members, but only criticisms that are genuinely felt and motivated by a wish to help the group to succeed in its task;
2. treat any critical comments about their ideas as constructive criticisms, rather than as personal attacks;
3. give any ideas or proposals made the same kind of critical scrutiny, regardless of the relative status of the proponent within the group;
4. share whatever relevant information they have that might help the group's work, and not assume too readily that relevant knowledge is held in common;
5. try to provide justifications for any proposals they make, so that their partners have a basis upon which to assess those proposals;
6. seek relevant information from other members, for example by asking if anyone has anything to share or add, and requesting that information is elaborated if it is not initially clear;
7. regularly seek ratification and check agreement for proposals that they make;
8. reflect together occasionally on their joint activity, focusing on such issues as whether they are following appropriate ground rules, if those rules need modification and if they are achieving a suitable balance between efficiency (not spending too much time in discussion) and effectiveness (allowing enough time for creative interthinking).

> *Class 7's ground rules*
>
> *When we work in a group ...*
>
> • Everyone offers relevant information
> • Everyone's ideas are treated as worthwhile - but are
>   critically evaluated
> • We ask each other questions
> • We ask for reasons and give them
> • We try to reach agreement
> • People trust each other and act as a team!

FIGURE 2.1   Ground rules for Exploratory Talk.

If group members behave in these ways, the discussion is likely to resemble Exploratory Talk, which we described in Chapter 1. Figure 2.1 is an example of ground rules for generating Exploratory Talk in the classroom, created by a teacher in one of our interventional studies.

One of the rules in Figure 2.1, 'We try to reach agreement', might seem problematic, given our earlier discussion of the need to avoid groupthink. Could this rule discourage the expression of some healthy disagreement? When describing our school-based research, we have sometimes been criticized for encouraging the inclusion of this rule, because, as critics commonly put it, surely we do not want to force agreement – cannot participants agree to disagree? The important thing here is to consider that particular ground rule in the context of the full set of rules (which are ultimately based on the definition of Exploratory Talk, as given in Chapter 1). On that basis, we would say this rule is not problematic and is in fact indispensable. Its true meaning is implied by its late position in the list: that after hearing and discussing critically all relevant information and ideas, a group should try to reach some conclusion as a basis for joint action. The value of this rule is that in requiring members of a group to seek a true, reasoned consensus, through discussion and debate, the risk of the kind of superficial agreement that typifies groupthink is more likely to be avoided. Although we have found no relevant evidence from research on adults, we might note that in her study of children's group work in mathematics and science problem-solving activities in school, Howe (2010) found that better solutions to problems, as well as better understanding and retention of subject knowledge, were achieved when children were expressly asked to try and reach agreement. What is more, the improved outcomes were found even when children in a group had failed to reach agreement: the important thing was that they had tried. This seeking of agreement seemed to encourage group members to 'go the extra mile' and critically evaluate any possible solutions, and so engage more deeply with the relevant knowledge.

Having drawn our general conclusions, we should not forget that different kinds of tasks may require different kinds of collaborative discussion. We can relate this claim to the three kinds of talk described in Chapter 1. For example, if members of a creative team agree that their task is, initially, to generate a list of possible names for a new brand of clothes, this might be best accomplished through a form of Cumulative Talk in which all ideas are accepted and elaborated but not criticized. This might avoid the premature narrowing of conceptual space that Middup *et al.* (*op. cit.*) identified as a problem, as discussed earlier. However, if they then had to select the best of these ideas as a basis for action, on the basis of feedback from possible retailers and customers and any other relevant information, then something resembling Exploratory Talk might be necessary.

Overall, then, it seems reasonable to conclude that there is no great discrepancy between the characteristics of creative, productive problem-solving discussions in the classroom and in the workplace, despite some important differences between those two social environments. In both types of situation, things seem to go awry when inappropriate ground rules are used, and/or when members are not all using the same ground rules. In both contexts, a discussion resembling Cumulative Talk may be very useful for initially sharing knowledge and generating new ideas; when conclusions have to be drawn, plans formulated and decisions made, discussion resembling Exploratory Talk is likely to be the best. The specific requirements of any task, or the stage reached in a task, will of course affect what is most productive at any time. It is hard to think of reasons for encouraging more Disputational Talk, though it is unlikely to become an endangered species. One can probably only expect it to be totally absent in discussions between emotion-free androids; but it would be likely to occur less often if members of working groups spent some time, initially, agreeing upon some suitable ground rules for their discussions.

3

INTERTHINKING AND THE PERFORMANCE ARTS

Introduction

In Chapter 2 we looked at the ways people can interthink in a variety of work situations. In this chapter, we focus on the importance of interthinking for human creativity. Some very strong support for the importance of collaboration in human creativity comes from biographical and literary studies of how exceptionally creative people in the arts and sciences have achieved their success. In recent times literary scholars have begun to question the accuracy of earlier biographies of famous writers, musicians and artists, which explained their success predominantly in terms of their individual talent and solitary endeavours. It is now widely held that those accounts commonly underestimated the influences of social contemporaries on their work. For example, Stone and Thompson (2006: 8–9) in their book *Literary Couplings*, suggest that the 'cult of the individual genius' that pervades many early accounts of the work of the Romantic writers (Wordsworth, Coleridge, Keats and their contemporaries) is based on a myth, because historical evidence shows that they relied heavily on collaborative support. Stillinger (1991) and Joffe (2007) likewise question the depiction of the talented author as a solitary genius who resists the influences of others, arguing that during their most productive periods successful writers typically belonged to specific communities, and/or worked in close relationships within which important new ideas and principles were generated and shared. For example, careful analysis has shown how the texts of the major works of Mary Shelley (author of *Frankenstein*) and her husband Percy Bysshe Shelley (author of 'Mont Blanc', 'Ozymandias' and other acclaimed poems) are not only interwoven, but draw heavily on their intense conversations about their shared experiences of living in the Alps, as reported in their personal journals (Mercer 2012). One can make similarly strong cases for the importance of collective thinking for the visual arts, music, scientific discovery and technological development. A very influential work on creative partnerships, combining perspectives and insights from both psychological and historical enquiry, is Vera John-Steiner's *Creative Collaborations* (2000). She offers a series of case studies of how people (mainly pairs, and often couples) have worked together to achieve significant success in the arts and sciences. Sometimes drawing on the collaborators' own reflective insights, John-Steiner shows that there are different ways that joint activity can be creative and productive; there is not just one successful model. Elsewhere, she makes a useful and interesting distinction between 'collaboration', 'cooperation' and 'social interaction', giving collaboration the highest status as 'an affair of the mind':

> Social interaction involves two or more people talking or in exchange, cooperation adds the constraint of shared purpose, and working together often provides coordination of effort. But collaboration involves an intricate blending of skills, temperaments, effort and some-times personalities to realise a vision of something new and useful.
>
> *(Moran & John-Steiner 2004: 11)*

While researchers such as Moran and John Steiner emphasize the importance of collaborative interaction for the realization of a creative vision, very little is known about the ways in which spoken language is implicated in collaborative creativity. Mindful of this, our own recent work has begun to explore creative interthinking by analyzing the talk of small groups of people composing, planning and rehearsing for musical performances. This focus highlights, at the interpersonal level, the role of interthinking and how it is implicated in the creative renewal of culture. Focusing on one particular domain of creative activity also enables us to examine, in depth, the ways talk is used in combination with other modes of communication, such as music itself. We begin by looking at discussions among bands of musicians in rehearsal, and then move on to see how collaborators from rather different disciplinary backgrounds – music, theatre, film and dance – work together to achieve an artistic product.

Collaborative creativity in musical rehearsals

We will first consider some research based on observations of jazz musicians improvising together, and then present the results of our own observations of other bands of musicians. We became interested in this kind of interthinking situation partly because one of us has an involvement in this kind of activity, giving us some initial insights into the ways it is organized. We also felt it provided a very suitable vehicle for understanding how a small group of people strive, over time, to generate an eventual artistic result with which they will all be clearly associated. In many other kinds of joint creative endeavour, there are visible and invisible contributors, obvious leaders and followers, people who come and go during an extended creative process. In the kinds of performing bands we have studied, the members all eventually stand up together on a stage and, in effect, say to their audience: 'We created this together; what do you think of it?' This may make these rehearsals different from some other kinds of creative collaboration we could have chosen, but it also means the interactive processes involved are more inclusive and, we think, more intense. In addition to this, because of the small numbers of people involved, and the fact that they are all present in each event, these processes are also easier to study than in more distributed kinds of collaboration.

Studies of collective rehearsal for musical performance are surprisingly rare, even though rehearsals are such an established and common feature of the musical world. With some notable exceptions, which we will consider, there has been very little research on collective musical activity that considers, in any systematic way, how musicians talk and interact. There seems to have been much more interest in composition as a solitary achievement (as discussed, for example, by Young 2008). Even though research on creativity now recognizes how it is commonly embedded in the interactions of continuing relationships and how creative products emerge from collaboration, very little is still known about the interthinking involved in the process. As two eminent researchers in the field have noted:

> The most substantial studies of group creativity have been social psychological studies of brainstorming groups ... but these studies have not analysed the interactional processes that occur within groups. This failure to analyse collaborative processes is a significant lacuna in creativity research because a wide range of empirical studies has revealed that significant creations are almost always the result of complex collaborations.
>
> (Sawyer & DeZutter 2009: 81)

The analysis we offer here is of a particular type of situation, but we hope that it will advance the understanding of the nature of collaborative music making and collaborative creativity more generally, even if not all that happens is generalizable. Our approach is based on sociocultural theory (as explained in Chapters 1 and 5) and we apply the methods of Sociocultural Discourse Analysis (described in Chapter 1), which emphasize the importance of the shared historical knowledge of communities (in this case, of musical genres and practices) and the importance of language and other communicative tools for pursuing and achieving common goals. We are particularly interested in how musicians use talk (and other modes of communication) in their rehearsals to interthink, drawing upon and developing their musical common knowledge. The disputes and conflicts that arise in the pursuit of their common goals can be particularly enlightening in that respect. We are also interested in how language is used in conjunction with other modes to generate a joint justification, or basis for confidence in the product, in preparation for a musical performance.

A sociocultural perspective on music rehearsals

We are expressly concerned here with the ways talk is used in the creation and rehearsal of music – but of course music is itself a particular cultural form of communication. Musicians, including some of those we have studied, also commonly use written notation (musical scores, charts and performance notes) to enable the coordination of their joint activities. Our analysis of rehearsals (as described in more detail in Littleton and Mercer 2012) shows very clearly that language is part of a multimodal toolkit for thinking collectively – a toolkit shaped by the needs of particular communities of practice. As we explained in Chapter 2, particular domains or communities of practice have generated distinctive language genres, and these have to be learned by novices. To understand collaborative musical creativity, it is necessary to examine not only the talk among band members but also the other modes of communication (including playing music) that are used to sustain such activity. The playing of music may not only be the end product of rehearsal, but also a mode of communication among band members that enables and sustains the rehearsal process.

How jazz musicians communicate while improvising

Fred Seddon (2004, 2005) studied how jazz musicians communicate while improvising in rehearsals and live performance, by observing and recording a group of six undergraduate student musicians over the course of six one-hour rehearsals and a live performance. He was particularly interested in

TABLE 3.1 Modes of communication among jazz musicians

Mode of communication	Verbal	Non-verbal
Instruction	Musicians are told what and when to play in pre-composed sections	Musicians learn pre-composed part by ear or read from music notation
Cooperation	Musicians discuss and plan the organization of the piece prior to performance in order to achieve a cohesive performance	Musicians achieve sympathetic attunement and exchange stocks of musical knowledge, producing cohesive performance employing body language, facial expression, eye contact, musical cues and gesticulation
Collaboration	Musicians discuss and evaluate their performance of the music in order to develop the content and/or style of the piece	Musicians achieve empathetic attunement and take creative risks that can result in spontaneous musical utterances; when they do, this signals empathetic creativity

(Adapted from Seddon 2004: 70)

how the individual musicians 'attuned' to each other, so as to achieve a successful collaborative performance. In his analysis, he distinguished between *verbal* and *non-verbal* means of communication, noting that non-verbal communication includes visual signals (such as a gesture to begin/end a sequence) as well as musical communication. He also found it useful to distinguish between talk being used for *instruction*, *cooperation* or *collaboration*, as set out in Table 3.1.

Some examples will make Seddon's analytic categories clearer. An example of *verbal instruction* was when one musician gave specific orders or guidance about what was expected to happen, without inviting any discussion as to how a piece should be performed – see, for example, Extract 3.1.

EXTRACT 3.1 Verbal instruction
Laura: Right, it's Pete and Chris playing what they just played . . .
Keith: Twice or . . . ?
Laura: Just once.

(From Seddon 2005: 53)

Verbal cooperative communication was more democratic talk about the organization of people's activity, such as what should happen and when. Extract 3.2 provides a good example:

EXTRACT 3.2 Verbal cooperation

Anthony: So what does it do . . . you know, when it gets into the solos?

Pete: Yeah . . . in between each solo you nod when you get to the last one.

Anthony: Yeah, yeah, yeah, but I mean, it goes erm . . . der . . . der der . . . der, der, der [sings phrase] . . . and you're straight in there, aren't you?

Pete: That's on the top – that der . . . der . . . der . . . is at the top of the solo, yeah.

(From Seddon 2005: 54)

Seddon made a distinction between 'cooperation' and 'collaboration' similar to that made by Moran and John–Steiner (*op. cit.*), as described earlier in this chapter. He described the verbal communication as *collaborative* when some 'higher order creative processes' seemed to come into play. In collaborative communication, performances were evaluated after completion, and creative changes were proposed and discussed; for example, see Extract 3.3.

EXTRACT 3.3 Verbal collaboration

Paul: I didn't think the feel worked for me in the solo . . . it doesn't really happen . . .

Chris: The blow [improvised solo playing] over it?

Paul: Well, just the whole feel of it . . . the whole . . .

Laura: I think maybe we could try it a bit quicker.

Chris: Yeah.

Anthony: Yeah.

Paul: You didn't want to swing it . . . did you or did you?

Keith: I don't think you would be able to swing it anyway. It would sound like a completely different tune . . .

(Seddon 2005: 54)

Seddon's analyses indicated that there was a link between the activity the musicians were engaged in and the mode of communication adopted. Instructional modes were typically used to initiate rehearsal of a piece, while cooperational modes were used to develop its cohesiveness. Generally, collaborative modes were used during the most creative phases of activity (Seddon 2004: 75).

Talk during the rehearsal of three bands

In our own studies, we have been especially interested in examining, in detail, the nature of what in Seddon's terms would be collaborative modes of communication, because this seems to be where the most productive interthinking happens – as band members worked on the creation of new musical compositions or new arrangements of existing ones. Our data has consisted of in-depth observations (captured in video-recordings/audio-recordings and field notes) of a series of rehearsals by three bands of musicians. All three bands were similar in that they played a form of 'non-classical', popular music and were working to create new, distinctive performance repertoires (which suited our interest in mutual composition as well as performance). That is, they were not aiming to perform accurate representations of existing pieces of music, or even existing musical arrangements, as would a classical ensemble or a popular music tribute or 'covers' band. They all were striving for a distinctive 'sound' in their performances (even when performing compositions created by others). They were also relatively democratic in structure, and their rehearsals offered some opportunity for improvisation and the renegotiation of arrangements. However, they did differ in some interesting ways. One of the bands consisted of five members, four male and one female aged about 15 years, and they played what was generally known at the time as 'indie' rock music. Their activities are discussed in more detail in Miell and Littleton (2008). The second band was made up of three male adult musicians (average age about 45) who were preparing to accompany the staging of a musical play. The third was a band of four members, three male and one female (average age about 52) who played acoustic country/roots music. Members of the first band were amateurs, while those of the two other bands were professionals or semi-professionals. To ensure confidentiality for our participants, we have changed the names in all transcripts and altered some other references to specific locations and events.

The three bands we studied were also chosen because we had established links with one or more members and this made access easier to what were essentially private events. Our selection criteria were not exacting, as this was an exploratory study; we simply wanted access to genuine rehearsals by small bands of musicians who were aiming for eventual public performance. In the case of the adult bands, we gathered data by 'sitting in' on rehearsals, by recording what was said on an audio-recorder, and taking notes about what went on to supplement the recordings. Occasionally, we interviewed band members about what was happening; but we do not draw on any of those interviews here. The amateur, teenage indie band were provided with a digital camcorder and asked to film all their band rehearsals leading up to and including their next gig. These rehearsals involved them not only bringing some pre-composed material to practise and/or develop but also using the sessions to compose new material collaboratively. The band members were encouraged to leave the camera recording throughout each session to capture the periods of both talk and music playing and also subsequently to discuss (to camera in video-diary style) their views of how the rehearsals were going and of the how they were working together to write and develop the material. This video-diary material is not, however, analyzed here.

The author of an earlier anthropological study of amateur/semi professional music making carried out in the same town as two of our case studies remarked on the enthusiasm and commitment of part-time musicians who gain little financial recompense for their efforts (Finnegan 2007). Our interest here is not in what reflective sense they made of what they were doing, but rather with how they negotiated the rehearsals as they happened. The strong impression that we gained from our observations was that the members of all three bands were highly engaged with the activity. Their commitment to repeatedly playing, replaying and reworking songs, both new and old, in an attempt to reach collectively agreed versions and interpretations, was impressive. This complex transactional process required band members to continually evaluate their own and each other's work. They regularly expressed their opinions, sometimes strongly, on how particular pieces were progressing. They also regularly offered ideas for improvement, modification and change as they played through pieces or reworked specific phrases. Members would frequently build musically on each other's ideas, playing through and exploring alternative versions and subtle variations. Of course, as in any working groups, participation was not equal, with some members being noticeably more vocal, or more assertive, than others. But they strived to resolve any differences of view, in order to reach a consensus to underpin their joint performance – as we will see from the examples below.

Extract 3.4, 'Not sure about the E', comes from a rehearsal session of the band preparing to accompany a musical play. It begins with the band members Norm, Peter and Kieran reviewing a particular piece of music that is to be played during a scene when characters interact, at times without speaking or singing. Norm played guitar, Peter keyboards and Kieran the bass. (There were other members of this ensemble, but they were not involved in this particular piece.) The play rehearsals had shown the scene to be of an uncertain duration, and so the required length of the piece of music was correspondingly uncertain. The piece of music they are rehearsing therefore had to function as an ambient accompaniment that could be halted or prolonged as the dramatic action required. Their immediate concerns in the extract were with how to segue from one section of the play to the next, and how to make sure the music could be sustained flexibly to match the duration of the scene. The band therefore needed a contingency plan for how to respond to the circumstances, as they emerged. A further complication was that the piece also had to provide a musical link from one song to the next, with the first song (sung before the piece) being in the key of G and the next (sung after the piece) in A. The composition of the piece had evolved, rather than being first formally written, in the course of the rehearsals. Aspects of it were thus still open to negotiation at the point the recording was made. It had been proposed that a transition through the chord of E major would help make the key shift, during the ambient phase, and it will be apparent that this proposal was still in dispute during Extract 3.4.

EXTRACT 3.4 Not sure about the E

Norm: We put the E in, it makes it slightly odd (*sounding worried*).

Peter: We've got to think in terms of words are concerned we only use, do that once at a time.

Norm: That's true.

Kieran: Yeh.

Peter: And then the, the long, the long A minors afterwards will simply be …

Norm: Yeh.

Kieran: Yeh, we can actually keep those cycling round as many times as we need to.

Norm: I'm not sure about the E (*still sounds unconvinced*).

Kieran: Right, OK.

Peter: I like it.

Norm: Yeh but except it's, because then you've got (*demonstrates on guitar*).

Peter: Yeh but hang on, I'm using G instead of E minor.

Norm: Yeh yeh, all right. Perhaps it works.

Kieran: Let's try that, it goes straight to the F (*they try it*).

Kieran: Yeh I think it actually works on the same number of bars because we're holding the F and G twice as long.

Norm: Yeh.

Peter: That's right.

The extract begins with Norm expressing his concern about the suitably of a chord – 'E major' – to enable the key transition, as previously proposed by Peter. His reasons appear to be musical – he doesn't like how E major sounds in relation to the chords that precede and succeed it. His colleagues seem less worried about this, with Peter suggesting that this is unimportant in the context of the piece as a whole. Kieran seems more concerned with the issue of sustaining the music for a suitable time. Norm and Peter then express very different views about the 'E' chord, and Norm explains his concerns with a musical demonstration of how he thinks the chord will sound in context. That is, he uses the music *rhetorically* – as musical evidence to support his spoken argument. This leads Peter to realize he had not been using the same chord as Norm before the 'E' (G major rather than E minor, which if played before E major creates a different effect, though the two chords have two notes in common). Kieran suggests they try using the G, which they do; and as a result a happy consensus is achieved.

In all the rehearsals we observed, the band members often expressed different points of view, and gave reasons to justify their particular preferences. Their interthinking was quite apparent in the talk; but, as in Extract 3.4, band members sometimes did so by using more than one communicative mode. Music was thus not only the product of joint activity, but also a vital medium (used in conjunction with language to generate persuasive communications) for negotiating that outcome. Sometimes it seemed to just be the collective appeal of the sound created that was critical, with relatively little explicit comment accompanying the apparent mutual recognition that something sounded 'right'.

The next sequence, Extract 3.5, comes from a rehearsal of the country/ roots band. Ivan is the main singer, and on guitar; Carl is also on guitar; Mac is on fiddle; Paula is on accordion; and Tom is on bass. As the extract begins, they have just run through a song in which the accordion has to come in with a distinctive and precise run of notes (what musicians often call a 'fill' or 'riff') at a certain point in each verse.

EXTRACT 3.5 A hard fill

(*The song has just ended and people begin to talk*)

Mac: (*To Paula*) It's a hard bloody fill for you to do, that, isn't it? I mean I wonder whether we . . .

Ivan: (*Interrupts*) But it sounds . . .

Carl: (*Interrupts*) When it works it's great.

Mac: I mean I would simplify it.

Tom: Yeah.

Mac: (*To Paula*) I mean I think we're asking an awful lot of you to do that (*laughs*) and I wonder if we shouldn't just do something simpler. You know, um.

Ivan: Well, for the first time out, trying in front of an audience, do something simple . . .

Mac: Yeah. Anyway, it's only an idea.

Paula: At the Canyon (*referring to a music venue*).

Ivan: . . . and then as we rehearse it more and more and get into it we increase the complexity . . .

Mac: I don't know what though, that's the point.

Ivan: . . . as you feel more comfortable.

Paula: It's only two weeks. What I need is a reminder. I'd forgotten about that one. Since I looked at it I haven't . . .

Ivan: Well how do you feel about it? Can you fit it in?

Paula: Um, I feel (*long pause*).

Mac: It's a tricky one, isn't it? To get it really sharp.

Paula: It's showing cos I haven't practised. This should ease up by the end of next week, I've got a, I've got a (*inaudible*).

Mac: (*Sings as plays notes of fill*) doo doo doo doooh. How about at the end of it, right, do the whole thing, slowly.

Paula: (*Plays original version of fill*)

Mac: You know (*plays just some of the notes*). If you could just do that.

Paula: If that fits in better (*plays same notes as simplified version of fill*).

Mac: (*To whole band*) Do it.
         (*Band plays whole section of song*)

Carl: Hmm, it's (*inaudible*) (*Some people still playing*)

Paula: It's, it's the rhythm of doing it, to be honest.

Mac: I mean, just do something much simpler. I just really feel it's too hard to fit it in really sharply. I mean for me on the fiddle that is a doddle (*plays it*) cos it's all open strings, and you know.

Paula: What's wrong, am I getting the rhythm wrong?

Mac: No. Sometimes. It's just sometimes it sounds like its slowing us down slightly when, you know, you know it doesn't seem like its kind of just keeping up. And . . .

Paula: To be honest, I haven't tried it since last week and therefore . . .

Ivan: (*Interrupts*) Could it just be three notes? (*Sings an arpeggio, D, B, F*)

Mac: I was just thinking that (*plays*). I mean the other, the simple thing to do could be to kind of, uh, the chords, the thirds. (*Plays a sequence of pairs of notes that is less complex than the 'fill' in question*) You know.
         (*This issue is not resolved, and the band move on to rehearse another tune*)

In this extract we see a delicate issue being raised and discussed, of a type which we quite commonly encountered in band rehearsals. It is whether, in the view one of the band members, one of the others is playing their part in a satisfactory way. In Extract 3.5 Mac raises this kind of issue with Paula, and pursues it somewhat relentlessly through the discussion. He argues that a less complex, 'simpler' series of notes might fill the slot in the arrangement better. Mac uses the terms 'simple/simpler/simplify' to repeatedly make this point. Ivan picks this terminology up and uses 'simple' once, though Paula never does, though she does admit that the rhythm of the fill is posing problems. Her position, it seems, is that she just needs more practice with the current arrangement to get it right. As in Extract 3.4, musical demonstration is used by band members in a rhetorical way to support their spoken argument. In this case, however, the argument is not carried by the demonstrations and the issue is not resolved. Nevertheless, this extract illustrates well how talk can be used in conjunction with other modes of communication by a group of people to interthink – making a problem explicit, reviewing it collectively, proposing creative solutions and jointly evaluating them. The problem raised in the extract was not solved in that one conversation, but that is not unusual in human endeavours. It is likely that the various band members stimulated by the discussion would go away and reflect on the problem and come back next time with new proposals. As we explained in Chapter 1 (and will discuss in more detail in Chapter 5), human thinking is characterized by the dynamic relationship between social interaction and individual cognition.

We observed that throughout rehearsals, band members were continually engaged in the joint evaluation and appraisal of their music. While the aim is to achieve a consensus as the basis for a performance, the interactions may nevertheless be highly emotive and confrontational, with particular individuals sometimes being singled out for criticism. We can see a rather extreme example of this in Extract 3.6, in an interaction between the teenage members of the rock band. As often in their rehearsals, comments made were often very direct and blunt, involving fierce critical commentary and frank assessment of the musical effects being achieved. Members sometimes engaged in what Storey and Joubert (2004: 46) have called 'lethal confrontations', in which they were intensely critical of each other's playing and creative contributions. In Extract 3.6, the band is working through a new piece and Dan is defending himself against Jack's accusatory comments that he is 'playing the wrong notes' and 'starting off on the wrong notes'.

EXTRACT 3.6 Wrong notes

Dan: Did you say I was playing the wrong notes?
Jack: Well yeah, maybe it just didn't sound right.
Leah: Play it through just the two of you.
Jack: Let's just play it . . .

Dan: I'm sure I was playing what I was playing before . . .

Jack: . . . and I'll tell you if it sounds right.

Dan: No it's not the tuning, it must be the notes but I was playing what I
        was playing before . . .

Jack: . . . Well you can't have been man . . .

Dan: . . . Well I am . . .

Jack: . . . We would have heard man . . .

Dan: . . . I swear, I swear.

Jack: You start off with a wrong note.

Dan: I'm not!

Jack: That's fucking . . . well it doesn't sound right does it!

Dan: Well that's what I was playing before.

Jack: Well we've got to do something new.

Dan: Play it right the way through.

Jack: It sounds shit man.

        (*The band try the same song again from beginning*)

The talk in Extract 3.6 might seem to bear more resemblance to
Disputational Talk than Exploratory Talk, with its assertions and counter-
assertions ('Well you can't have been man'; 'Well I am'), but it also has
some Exploratory Talk features. Partners ask each other questions, and offer
justifications for their statements and actions ('No it's not the tuning, it
must be the notes'; 'We would have heard it man'), and in general seem to
be seeking a consensus, which will help them achieve their joint goal ('Well
we've got to do something new'). Despite the intensity of the interactions,
the collaboration between the band members did not break down in, or
after, these violent clashes. Such episodes of Disputational Talk did not
cause any lasting damage to their working relationship and sometimes after
these conflicts creative 'breakthroughs' seemed to happen, or they set off
on subsequent useful rounds of re-working and re-playing (as was the case
here). The collective sense of something 'working' was often hard won and
the consensus achieved at times seemed fragile, and not equally supported
by the collaborators.

   As noted earlier, all three of the bands studied were, to varying extents,
working in an improvisational manner, rather than seeking to achieve
canonical performances as is the case within the classical tradition. The
multimodal aspect of their activity was also represented in the way that the
theatre band and the roots band worked from a combination of written
music and 'charts' (which included the main chords, aspects of arrangements
and various performance notes emerging from the rehearsals). The rock band
also referred to chords and agreed arrangements, but were not looking for

any one existing style to 'fit into'. Instead they drew on various established musical genres, experimenting with and borrowing from them in order to forge and define their own distinctive sound. This aim of creating a distinctive group sound was commonly invoked in their rehearsal talk, as in Extract 3.7.

EXTRACT 3.7 Bit too funky

Jack: That bit's just not sounding right … It's sounding a bit too, like, I don't know a bit too funky almost, in a way.
Matt: I don't know, it changes the vibe a bit.
Jack: Changes?
Matt: Just the mood of the band.
Jack: I know but that's not necessarily a good thing.
Matt: Yeah I know.

This extract illustrates well how these kinds of creative collaborations rely on much implicit understanding on the part of collaborators. In Extract 3.7, sounds that change the vibe and the mood of the band are rejected as 'not right', even though they might have some merit in principle, because it is agreed that they are not in keeping with the distinctive style of music being forged by the band.

Collaboration across art forms

In Chapter 2 we discussed Anne Edwards' research on interprofessional work, in which two or more people from different occupational backgrounds were trying to accomplish something together, drawing on their different fields of expertise. We can consider the same kind of issue here, by drawing on recent research by Elizabeth Dobson (2012) who studied creative arts students working together. The research was undertaken while she studied for her doctorate with one of us at the Open University (see also Dobson, Flewitt, Littleton and Miell 2011). It focused on the activities of four undergraduate students (variously specializing in theatre, dance, digital video and music technology), over a period 12 weeks, as they worked to compose a ten-minute film, which would include music and dance. Taking a similar sociocultural perspective to our own, she was interested in how the students used the cultural tools of language and computer-based technology to pursue their common goals.

In Chapter 2 we alluded to the ways that, with particular communities of practice based on an occupation of field of knowledge, the efficiency of collaboration can be greatly assisted by participants all being fluent in the same genres and technical terms, and able to invoke shared background knowledge through brief references. Within their respective domains of knowledge, pairs of students in Dobson's research were able to use highly technical language in that easy and efficient way, as Extract 3.8, involving two music students (Liam and John), shows.

EXTRACT 3.8 Familiarity between peers

Liam: Maybe it would be a good idea for us to go up for a session and for you to observe me working on my sonic arts piece. How I'm using the plug-ins.
        [I just need to show you]
John: [Oh that sounds like my idea] of hell.
Liam: Ok then we need to t . . .
John: You know how impatient I am.
Liam: No but just so that cos you already know Cubase so you'll be able to use (*unintelligible*)
John: Yeh yeh Nuendo'll be fine yeh.
Liam: You'll be fi absolutely fine with it.
John: Er[m]
Liam: [But] that means you can go off and work on your own.
John: Sure definitely. I mean what I would like to do is, like I say is, write scores and go up there and work together to those scores.

(Adapted from Dobson op. cit.: *159)*

We can see in Extract 3.8 the students' implicit appeals to each other's technical knowledge in their brief references to types of musical recording software (Cubase and Nuendo). However, they did not necessarily have all relevant knowledge in common to enable them to work effectively together. One of the issues Dobson explored was how the students from different backgrounds overcame communicative problems caused by their divergent sources of knowledge and experience. They had not worked together before, and did not have a shared frame of reference on which to base their project. They needed to create a new 'common knowledge' and some effective ways of talking about it, in order to pursue their joint activity. This process of developing a basis for shared understanding inevitably took some time, but it could be seen to be happening, in different ways, in the specific interactions that Dobson recorded. Sometimes it was simply a matter of one partner asking for some information that they lacked but was necessary for pursuing their collaboration. In Extract 3.9 the music student Liam asks the dance specialist Kath about the space needed for a performance. As you read it consider how well Kath seems to respond to Liam's request.

EXTRACT 3.9 Knowledge of collaborators and interactional choices

Liam: How much of, oh sorry, er, how much of space do you use when you're doing dance, or how much you thinking if you've got like a room is it very static or does it move round quite a bit?
Kath: It depends.
Liam: Yeh.
Kath: Like I'm choreographing a solo now.
Liam: Yeh.
Kath: That's like literally like all on one spot, I'm not gonna move off . . .
Liam: Yeh.
Kath: . . . a square
Liam: Yeh.
Kath: but you can use any space really.
Liam: Yeh.

(Adapted from Dobson op. cit.: 149)

You may agree with us that Kath does not seem to give a very explicit, informative response; though the real test would be what sense Liam made of it. In comparison, Dobson provides this example (Extract 3.10) of the students she studied establishing some common ground by sharing their ideas in an open, uncritical way.

EXTRACT 3.10 Cumulative talk: knowledge sharing and creating

Di: I think at the end like you should s- like s- s- something like a scream or something like d'ye know when they like in a space and then its like really weird [but then]
Kath: [I think] laughter I think laughter's quite creepy
Di: [Yeh]
Kath: (*unintelligible*)
Di: And then like a, d'ye know when it like sends shivers down your spine, stuff, like spine and then they've just got to leave through the set like the tunnel of the set we made.
John: Yeh. Is there any particular like words erm
Kath: Yeh I already said that didn't I?
Di: Foliage, [fo, what's]
John: [Some sort of]
Kath: What did you say? Is there any words?
John: Yeh I don't know like poems or something you know, something, something that suits the

Kath: Yeh I said that didn't I, that it would be really cool to have like one, everything like there's no speech but then there's like one line that you just say.

John: We can do some quite cool processing with speech . . .

(Adapted from Dobson op. cit.: 162)

In Chapter 1 we described the three kinds of talk that we and our colleagues used to describe the various ways schoolchildren talked while working in groups – *Disputational*, *Cumulative* and *Exploratory*. In her analysis, Dobson identifies much of the talk in these 'common knowledge building' sequences as Cumulative, because the participants were sharing ideas and information in an open, uncritical way. At first, this mainly consisted of the provision of relevant information, sometimes in response to a query, as in Extract 3.6 above. However, as the project progressed, she noticed that this Cumulative Talk began to invoke the history of the collaboration. She comments, 'In Cumulative Talk, contributions were retroactive and contingent on everything that had already been offered' (270). She also noticed that, as they referred to what had jointly been said and done already, 'the students were continually developing and enriching prior contributions' (270). That is, the talk embodied both the past and the future of the students' shared experience. It was therefore possible to see it creating a temporal framework to support the pursuit of interthinking and collective activity.

Talk and creative interthinking

We began the chapter by presenting an analysis of some specific events within a certain kind of practice. Even within the field of musical performance, the rehearsals we have discussed may not be representative of the processes involved in creative collaboration in the arts. As we mentioned at the beginning of the chapter, some artistic collaborations do not require all the creative participants to be present at any one time. Within a creative team, there may be a more obvious authoritative role for one person, or all participants may not have to formally identify with the final product (for example, in the making of a film, or the performance of a play or a piece of classical music). However, we suggest that some generalities can be identified. One is that any such collective creative activity is necessarily predicated on the shared historical knowledge of communities (in our particular case, of musical genres, notations and practices) and the use of language as a cultural and psychological tool. Moreover, that tool is commonly used in conjunction with other communicative tools. We saw how the musicians we observed used musical performance as a rhetorical tool, along with spoken language, to convince band members of their point of view. Understanding the ways different modes or tools are used in harmony in any artistic domain helps us see how collaboration is pursued in any particular domain of creative activity.

We have also illustrated the potential significance of conflict or tension for successful creative collaboration, which we also suggest is of general relevance. Other researchers have also highlighted its function in stimulating a successful result (Eteläpelto & Lahti 2008). Discussing what research tells us about creative collaboration in general, Moran and John-Steiner (2004) conclude that emphasizing the maintenance of consensus, rather than giving active consideration to multiple perspectives, tends to depress creativity. This should make us question any of our implicit assumptions about what is a 'good' collaborative relationship. While aesthetic disagreements about a joint venture can of course be disruptive, and seem to be a common reason for bands of musicians to split up, can a successfully creative collaboration be totally free of any conflict? If at least part of the general nature of collective artistic activity is accurately represented by our analysis, then it is clear that we cannot understand such activity without understanding the communicative processes inherent in it, and their functions.

The three types of talk

Our analysis of the rock band's rehearsal in Extract 3.6 led to the conclusion that their talk had features of both Disputational Talk and Exploratory Talk. It was disputational in that assertions sometimes met with counter-assertions, and the general tenor of the talk seemed at times confrontational rather than collaborative. But it also had features of the kind of reasoned discussion associated with Exploratory Talk, with questions asked, justifications being offered and proposals being made for how to resolve the problem. It was also interesting to see Dobson giving Cumulative Talk such an important role as the creation of dynamic common knowledge, because in the typology of the three types of talk, Cumulative Talk (given its uncritical, sharing nature) can easily be perceived as the 'poor relation' of Exploratory Talk (with its cut-and-thrust of challenges and justifications).

In her research on children aged 13–14 using computer-based technology to create music together, Dillon (2004) observed partners pursuing very creative collaborations through using talk of a more cumulative kind, which lacked the critical challenge of Exploratory Talk. She suggests that the archetypal form of Exploratory Talk may be more associated with success in logical, 'closed' problem-solving situations rather than in more 'open' creative endeavours such as making new music. Our own research with colleagues on collaborative creativity (Vass, Littleton, Miell & Jones 2008; Rojas-Drummond, Littleton, Hernandez & Zúñiga 2010) has led to the same conclusion. A situation where one of the 'ground rules' for talk is 'ideas will be heard and registered without criticism' can be very useful, especially at certain stages of joint creative activity – for example, when a task is first being considered and a group has to decide what knowledge they should share that might be relevant. Cumulative Talk may also often be useful when, after some extended Exploratory Talk discussions, a group is simply trying to record what they have achieved and what has been agreed. At such points, one may sometimes see talk of an 'exploratory' kind shifting to become more 'cumulative'. If Cumulative talk is seen as the poor relation of Exploratory Talk, in this metaphorical family Disputational talk is the grumpy time-waster. It may be that it can also serve some useful functions, for example in highlighting points of disagreement, or allowing participants to 'let off steam' before they return to working more collaboratively, as in Extract 3.6 earlier in the chapter. But is more likely to represent obstructive rather than constructive interaction.

We suggest, then, that the typology of the three types of talk has value for understanding group processes beyond the situations involving children in classrooms from which it emerged. Moreover, that usefulness is not undermined by the fact that actual examples of talk may not fit neatly into one or other of the three types. As we explained in Chapter 1, the typology is not meant to represent precisely the range of ways spoken language can be used for interthinking. Rather, it is a heuristic tool for appreciating the functional variety of talk. The three-part typology provides a useful initial framework for understanding how talk is used for interthinking because it focuses on the extent to which, and how effectively, partners are sharing their knowledge resources and reasoning about their joint task. Other kinds of distinctions, such as those between instructional, cooperative and collaborative forms of communication made by Seddon (*op. cit.*) as discussed earlier, may well be better suited to the pursuit of some concerns – such as his special interest in how individuals contribute to collaborative performances. Methods for making any specific and precise analyses of language in use need be designed to answer the relevant research questions.

Different modes of communication

Early in the chapter, we described how Seddon attended to verbal and non-verbal modes of communication between musicians. One example of non-verbal communication he identified was the use of 'musical cues' during a performance, whereby jazz musicians used their actual performance to signal to each other, so as to coordinate their activities. Music can thus have communicative functions beyond that normally associated with it, which is the generation by a musician of an emotional or intellectual response in a listening audience. Our own research has shown that music offers additional resources for interthinking, because it may also be used rhetorically, to make (or at least support) an argument (see, or example, Extract 3.4). In this way, we see how the spoken mode of language and another mode of communication can be employed in harmony.

The linguist Gunther Kress (2010) has taken a leading role in describing the multimodal nature of human communication. He suggests that different modes – visual and auditory forms of non-verbal communication as well as spoken and written language – have inherent *affordances*. By this he means that particular modes may be particularly well suited to convey certain kinds of meanings or messages. The visual mode of drawing, for example, is very well suited for communicating the relative position and distance of places on a landscape, as on a map. As in the rehearsals we described earlier, singing or playing is much better than words or any written notation for quickly demonstrating how a tune might sound. Within the practices of particular communities, modes acquire special *functions*. In law, for example, it is normal to use the spoken mode to make arguments (as in court cases), but only agreements consolidated in the written mode are likely to be treated as binding (as in contracts). Used in combination, modes thus represent related options for 'making signs' – or rather, making meaning. We can make a comparison between two modes, talk and music, as presented in Table 3.2. Included are some illustrative affordances and functions of each, from our study of rehearsals.

Two kinds of common knowledge

As in all conversations, the talk in a band rehearsal relies on the establishment of a base of common knowledge and necessarily involves the extension of that base. Band members in a rehearsal use language to travel together on their joint endeavour from the past into the future, continually transforming the current state of their understanding of what they are about and where they are going. To do so, they need to build a contextual foundation for their talk; and they use talk to build that contextual foundation. Gee and Green (1998) refer to this aspect of language use as 'reflexivity'. If one is interested in how talk is used to enable joint creative activity, one must be concerned with the reflexivity of dialogue, and a concern with how knowledge is developed as a joint resource over time.

TABLE 3.2 Talk and music as modes of communication for joint activity

Mode	Talk	Music
Affordances	Explicit presentation of ideas	Expression of tonal and temporal relations
	Flexible adaptability to specific contexts and to shared, specialized purposes of a community	Flexible adaptability to specific contexts (such as those of specific ensembles) and to shared, culturally-based aesthetic norms and conventions
Special functions (in band rehearsal settings)	Management of social relations	Demonstration of proposed musical features
	Invocation of past shared experiences	Testing of musical ideas in practice
	Direct instruction by one participant of others	Demonstration of problematic aspects and possible solutions
	Presentation of plans and arguments for change	Demonstrations of 'correct' performance by one participant to another
	Rhetorical efforts to pursue individual goals	Cues to action, to help others know what to do
	Accountability for performance	

If a group of people who are striving for some joint creative achievement engage in a series of meetings, the cognitive and social resources they need are gradually accumulated and refined. We have seen that within such meetings, some process of reflective review will normally also take place. Dobson's research, because it followed the activities of a group over a period of 12 weeks, offered some very valuable insights into this important, temporal aspect of interthinking. One of the key concepts she identifies is 'common knowledge' – what the group members come to know in common. We can take this a little further, by suggesting that successful participation in the rehearsals and performance of a musical group draws on two kinds of common knowledge. There is the kind that is accumulated through the activities of a group, whereby participants begin to appreciate their role in relation to others, perhaps learning to adapt their style to fill the 'space' they are given (and taking account of the personalities involved). We might call this *dynamic common knowledge*, because it emerges from the dynamics of the group's own extended activity. This dynamic common knowledge also includes their growing understanding of the particular pieces they are rehearsing and any aesthetic criteria that have been discussed and, hopefully, agreed. Dobson's research showed how important the kind of discussion we call Cumulative Talk is for enabling the creation of this new kind of common knowledge. However, the success of any ensemble – and probably of most creative collaborations – also depends on what we might call *background common knowledge*, which is that which any established member of a community of practice can take for granted as being shared with other members of that community, and so does not need to be explained from first principles when two such members are working together. Background common knowledge underpins fluency in a specialized technical discourse, and so enables the kind of discussion we saw two of Dobson's students pursuing in Extract 3.8, earlier in this chapter (when they assumed each other's knowledge of Cubase and Nuendo). It draws on certain levels of skill and understanding gained before, outside, the current activity. As Sawyer puts it:

> Many people think that jazz musicians play whatever comes into their heads in a burst of unconstrained inspiration. But even the freest improviser plays within a musical tradition, and before you can improvise you have to learn that tradition.
>
> *(Sawyer 2012: 337)*

Seddon's study of jazz musicians, discussed earlier, highlights the link between the two kinds of knowledge. For the improvisation to work well, the band members must be able to trust each other's background knowledge and skill, so that they can concentrate on their own performance. They also have to learn what each performer is able to add to the ensemble, so that each player can work in harmony with the others. Seddon calls the development of this kind of dynamic common knowledge, which has an emotional as well as a conceptual quality, 'empathetic attunement' (Seddon 2004, 2005).

Although it is useful to distinguish, conceptually, dynamic background knowledge from background common knowledge, the two kinds of shared information will not remain separate in the activity of any group. Some new knowledge or skills generated by a group's activities may, over time, become a common resource for activity within the group, or even become consolidated into the knowledge resources of their community of practice. The background knowledge of some group members may need to be explained and shared explicitly with other members, as in the interdisciplinary groups studied by Dobson.

Concluding remarks

In this chapter we have explored the processes of creative interthinking in the context of music rehearsals and an interdisciplinary creative arts project. The analyses presented reveal the ways in which ideas are explored, evaluated and developed over time through talk. They also show how other modes of communication have an important role to play in enabling individuals to think creatively together; but these analyses support the view we expressed in Chapter 1, that language is the primary mode for such intermental activity. Through the analytic work presented we see, once again, the value and significance of Exploratory Talk for the development and evaluation of ideas. The analyses presented also indicate how, in the interplay of dynamic and background common knowledge, an ever-expanding foundation of shared understanding is constituted – understanding that will carry the weight of subsequent, future dialogue, contribute to a continuity of experience and become the contextual basis for onward collaboration and interthinking.

4

DIGITAL TECHNOLOGY AND INTERTHINKING

Introduction

Much has been written about the ways that electronic, digital technology can 'transform' or 'revolutionize' interpersonal communications. This is not mere hyperbole. People can now communicate quite easily with other individuals far away, send each other various kinds of multimodal information and organize group events and collective creations without being ever in the same room as other participants. Both of us, the authors, have written articles with co-authors we have never met and would not recognize on the street. Terms such as 'transformation' and 'revolution' have also been used to make claims about the effects of that same technology on education. Again, there is some justification for such claims. Distance education is now possible on a level of scale and accessibility its pioneers could hardly have imagined; and the ubiquity of PCs, laptops, tablets and interactive whiteboards (all connected to the internet) in classrooms would probably astonish even a computer scientist of the early 1960s.

However, there is a danger that the wealth of communicative facilities offered by digital technology distracts us all from concerns about the quality of communication. A clear line on the telephone never ensured that two speakers would have a conversation in which they understood each other well, and the added visual dimension offered by Skype will not do so either. Computers in their various forms, and their software, are cultural tools that we employ well or badly. They can certainly make interthinking possible between people who would otherwise have been separated, and they can provide practical and very useful support for groups of people who are working and learning together. However, the issues we have raised in previous chapters concerning how people use language and other modes of communication to create knowledge together cannot be transcended by technology. It is from this perspective that, in this chapter, we will consider how digital technology can help interthinking processes.

One of our enduring research interests has been in how the kinds of computer-based technology that are available in schools can be used to help children engage productively in dialogue. Recently, with several colleagues, we have examined how the interactive whiteboard might be used for this purpose, and we will describe what we have found in the early part of the chapter. One of the most important and obvious contributions that digital technology might make to the processes of interthinking is to enable people who are in distant locations to do so, through enabling them to communicate online. We will discuss that kind of use of computer-mediated communication in the later part of the chapter.

A new everyday technology in the classroom: the interactive whiteboard

The interactive whiteboard (IWB) is now an almost universal fixture in every classroom in UK schools, where it has replaced the older technology of the blackboard – literally so, being typically placed on the wall behind the teacher's desk at the head of the classroom. Originally created for use in business settings (as is the case with virtually all the technology used in schools), it has been redesigned to enable the presentation, manipulation and annotation of images, text and video on a large touch-sensitive screen. Commercially-prepared educational resources can be presented on it, but teachers can also create and present their own multimedia resources, and annotate such presentations in the course of a lesson. Material generated and presented on it during a lesson can be saved and used again on subsequent occasions. Unlike the PC or laptop, the IWB has features that make it suitable for supporting the activity of an adult teaching a class of children; but, except for the research we will describe next, little attention has been given to its use in the collaborative learning of a small group of students.

One of us was involved in a project on IWBs with colleagues Ruth Kershner, Paul Warwick and Judith Kleine Staarman (described in more detail in Mercer, Kershner, Warwick and Kleine Staarman 2010; Warwick, Mercer and Kershner 2013), carried out in primary schools in the Cambridge area. It is an established practice in British primary education for children to work in small groups (without the constant presence of the teacher), so we used that as the basis for our project. With a group of primary school teachers, it was agreed that during group work sessions, one group of children within each class would use the IWB as the main resource for their work on habitats, as part of their study of science. The teachers were introduced to the practical findings of relevant research, including our own, on enabling and supporting children's collaborative learning, groupwork and interthinking. We then recorded a short series of lessons in each of the 12 classes (of children aged between seven and 11 years) of the six participating teachers. The activities carried out by the children were designed by the teacher in conjunction with the researchers, but were based on the usual science curriculum. Other children in the same class carried out essentially the same activities, but without using the IWB. We thus gathered observational data on the activities of 12 groups of children working at the IWB, but we will only use examples from one class here. The following two extracts were recorded during one science lesson in one of the classrooms we observed. We will use the examples from this class to illustrate the conclusions we drew from observing all six classes about how the affordances of the IWB can help children carry out a joint learning activity.

In the first extract (Extract 4.1), a group of three children (who we will call Leonie, Gordon and May) were involved in a lesson about animals and their adaptation to different habitats. The task they were working on required them to identify the features of an unknown creature, make notes about it and choose a suitable habitat for it. Their conclusions were expected to be supported by reasons, generated and agreed through their group discussion. They were then asked to identify features of other animals (such as polar bears and giraffes) that help them survive well in their own habitat, and in a plenary to discuss questions related to this (for example, why they would not find a polar bear living in a desert). As expected from our planning, the teacher began the lesson by drawing the attention of all the children in the class to the ground rules for discussion that had previously been agreed and were intended to encourage the use of Exploratory Talk (as defined in Chapter 1).

The teacher set up the IWB-based group activity by arranging a set of slides in a specific order to structure the task. The first of these was a picture of an imaginary creature, the Gruffalo (using an illustration by Axel Scheffler, taken from the book *The Gruffalo* by Julia Donaldson), and also included a set of possible habitats (desert, woodland, etc.) in which the Gruffalo could be located. The lesson began with an introduction, in which the teacher used the IWB to explain the task to the whole class. On the screen was a picture of the Gruffalo. The teacher moved to the next slide on the IWB, which suggested that an unusual creature had been discovered and that the children's task was to find out as much as they could about the creature. They were asked to look carefully at the physical features of the Gruffalo and think about their possible functions. They were also asked to think about the Gruffalo's diet and how it moved.

After about five minutes of whole-class discussion in which the teacher checked that the children understood the task, all the children started working on it in their groups. Only one group worked at the IWB, and it is that group we will focus on here. The class's agreed ground rules for talk were clearly visible on a display to the group working at the IWB, while cards listing the rules were on the tables of each of the other groups. Those groups were also given an illustration of an imaginary animal for their consideration.

As they were already familiar with the Gruffalo and knew that it lived in a wood, the children might well have had preconceived ideas about its habitat, which might potentially limit the scope of their discussion. However, the essence of the task was that they were required to give *reasons* for their views; they could not simply assert that something was the case. Indeed, the fact that they may have been familiar with the creature could have made this task more demanding, as they needed to consider the Gruffalo from a more objective, scientific perspective.

As Extract 4.1 starts, the three children are standing in front of the IWB. On it is a large picture of the Gruffalo. Down the right-hand side of the screen is a menu list of 'thumbnail' versions of all the relevant slides, which can be brought to the main screen by touching them. The teacher has asked them to use the IWB pen to write next to the picture of the Gruffalo what distinctive features it has, and what functions these might perform.

EXTRACT 4.1 The features of the Gruffalo

May: I think it's got horns, what do you think its got horns for?

Leonie: Horns for head-butting its prey.

May: Maybe, or maybe for having a fight with another male?

Gordon: Knobbly knees.

Leonie: For what though, what can you use them for?

May: Knobbly knees for, knobbly knees for uh protecting itself from kneeling on sharp stones.

Gordon:	What does he need a big black tongue for?	
May:	Um to make it look scary.	
Leonie:	No in the book it says it's sticky.	
Gordon:	Yeah but we're not reading the book, it's what you can see.	
Leonie:	I know, but then we know it's sticky.	
Gordon:	From what you can see.	
May:	How does it move? Um something for how does it move?	
Leonie:	No look, there's the stuff. 'How does it move, how does it eat? What does it eat?'	*Leonie reads the questions which the teacher pinned on the wall*
May:	What, what could it eat?	
Leonie:	We don't know what it eats.	
Gordon:	It's got a black tongue, so it would be something black probably.	
May:	Or something sticky?	
Leonie:	Flies, flies.	
Gordon:	Yeah probably flies and wasps or something.	
Leonie:	No not wasps, they'll sting him.	
Gordon:	So what?	
Leonie:	Big black tongue, sticky tongue, write sticky tongue. Big black sticky tongue to, to eat flies, to catch flies on its tongue.	*Leonie points to where she has earlier written 'big black tounge' [sic]. Gordon adds the word 'sticky' and then 'to catch flys' [sic]*
Leonie:	To catch flies. That's not how you spell it, its FLI.	*Leonie takes the pen and rewrites 'flies'*
May:	No it's not!	
Leonie:	Yes it is! It is.	
May:	Oh yeah.	
Gordon:	Are you sure?	
Leonie:	Flies, yeah it is.	

May: Well it's not how you spell it here.
Leonie: Flies, when you fly something it's
           Y, but when you fly, like flies the
           animal, it's FLIES
May: OK.
           (Adapted from Mercer, Warwick, Kershner & Kleine Staarman 2010)

In this extract we can see that all three children are fully engaged in their task. They share relevant information, ask for each other's views ('What do you think it's got horns for?') and offer constructive suggestions for joint consideration ('Um, to make it look scary.'). They constructively challenge each other's ideas and engage in productive argument (as illustrated by the sequence that begins with Gordon's remark: 'What does he need a big black tongue for?'). Leonie and Gordon disagree, but both offer reasons and justifications for their views. Their interaction thus has several key characteristics of Exploratory Talk. Towards the end of the extract, the argument that ensues is about spelling rather than the substantive activity topic, and becomes a little more 'disputational' ('No, it's not!' 'Yes, it is!'), but it is still on task and includes reasoned justifications. The tenor of the interaction, which cannot be ascertained from the transcript, was never angry or dismissive, but friendly throughout. The extract is not an ideal example of Exploratory Talk, by any means – Leonie has clearly the most assertive voice in the debate – but at the end of their animated discussion, in which various points of view were contested, they had produced the kind of joint documentation the teacher had hoped for. This activity took place quite early in these children's involvement with ground rules for talk, and so the signs that its features are starting to appear in their discussion is encouraging.

So how did the IWB figure in this interaction? It made a very useful contribution in a number of simple and quite functional ways, not least that it was simultaneously the source of information about the Gruffalo and the notebook in which they captured their emerging ideas. We can see from Figure 4.1 that the children made numerous notations on the board. By capturing key ideas from the ephemerality of talk, in a format that is easily amended and manipulated, it helped them to keep track of the diversity and interplay of ideas as they thought through the task together. Of course, the activity could also be carried out using more conventional resources such as the Gruffalo book, a worksheet and pen and paper, as indeed was the case for the groups of children in the class who were working without the IWB. However, none of those groups was so easily able to consider and debate the characteristics of the Gruffalo, review what they had jointly written about

FIGURE 4.1   The children working at the interactive whiteboard.

them against the empirical evidence and then modify what they had written after discussion. Any technology that enables interthinking to become more dynamic and efficient in such ways is, in our view, a good idea.

Extract 4.2 comes from a point in the same activity when the children have been exploring whether a woodland habitat would be an appropriate one for the Gruffalo. The children have already identified some well-suited positive aspects of such a habitat for the Gruffalo. They are now at the point when the woodland scene is shown, with the Gruffalo standing in the middle of it (shown in Figure 4.1).

EXTRACT 4.2 Finding a habitat

Leonie:	(*To May*) Don't write it too big. That's it, that's the right size.	*May is writing on the screen, across the picture of*
May:	Good camouflage.	*the Gruffalo in the wood,*
Leonie:	Good cover.	*while Leonie and Gordon*
May:	I know, camouflage.	*watch*
Leonie:	(*Spelling out*) Oh, A. M.	
May:	I know how to spell it. OK I don't know how to spell it.	
Leonie:	CAMAFLA.	

May:	No, it's O.	
May:	Camouflage, GE.	
Gordon:	Camouflage, its camouflage.	
Leonie:	Cam – ouflage, no because you don't.	
May:	No camouflage, and lots of um.	
Leonie:	I know what I'm writing. I'm writing good source of food under rocks.	
May:	(*Speaking as she writes*) Lots of animals for food.	*May is writing 'lots of animals'*
Leonie:	I'm writing ...	
Gordon:	Just write lots of animals. Looks like one big word, lots of animals. (*Laughs*)	
Leonie:	Lots – of – animals – for – food.	(*Leonie reads what May writes*)
Leonie:	No, I'm going to put good source of food under rocks.	*May gives the pen to Leonie*
May:	Yeah you won't expect to find deer under rocks.	*Leonie gestures writing in the air with the pen as she speaks*
Leonie:	Good source of food.	
Gordon:	Shall we write ... ?	
Leonie:	(*Interrupting*) No good source of food under rocks like ... and then I'll write.	*Leonie climbs on the box, and begins writing at the very top of the screen and speaking what she writes. Gordon gestures writing as he says 'e.g. blah ...'. Leonie wobbles and May holds her against the board to steady her. All laugh*
Gordon:	e.g. blah, blah, blah.	
Gordon:	Don't hold on to it, it's going to go bang!	
Leonie:	Um good. Good source of, good source of food under.	
Gordon:	Rocks, e.g.	*She begins to write, occasionally rubbing out and rewriting, and using different hands to make the pen reach different parts of the screen. Gordon and May then stand or wander around her, watching as she writes slowly. This takes several minutes*
Leonie:	Um ants, e.g. um ants.	
May:	Ants, bugs.	
Gordon:	Ants, termites.	
Leonie:	Ants.	
May:	Ants, bugs, termites.	
Leonie:	Wo, wo. Ants.	
May:	Termites. TE.	
Leonie:	Ter, oh right.	

May: TER mites. I've got a headache. Termites, bugs.
Leonie: Termites and bugs and um, leaves, there would be loads of leaves.
Gordon: And why do they need leaves?
May: Oh yeah, there's probably leaves under rocks.
Gordon: You wouldn't go termites and bugs and leaves and trees and blah, blah, blah.
Leonie: Yeah, termites. Ants, termites.
Gordon: And bugs. That's fine.   *They start to write this on*
                                                       the IWB

(Adapted from Mercer, Warwick, Kershner & Kleine Staarman 2010)

The manner and content of the children's talk as they begin their task indicates that they are very concerned about the quality of what they write on the board – that the writing is not too big, that it does not contain spelling mistakes and so on. They seem to regard what they write as being for public display, rather than informal notes as their teacher intended. There is a lot of instruction from the others to whoever is the scribe. It is not Disputational Talk, but nor is it the reasoned discussion of Exploratory Talk. Nevertheless, as the discussion progresses they pursue the key task – that of recording features of the woodland habitat that they think will suit the Gruffalo. They continually make suggestions, offering each other advice concerning what to write on the IWB and how to spell it – advice that is typically valued and acted upon. Their talk exhibits some features of what we have called Cumulative Talk.

Cumulative Talk can be very appropriate at this late stage in a task, when partners are working to produce an agreed written outcome from their prior discussion. The children add ideas and contributions through accumulation and accretion – each of the pupils speaking out loud what they wish to write on the board and each taking a turn to do so. The dialogue does not have many 'exploratory' features, though we should note Gordon's final query about 'leaves' generates a short discussion, which appears to result in consensus. The important point here, in any case, is not whether Leonie, Gordon and May do or do not succeed in collaborating well, but that our analysis of their talk (as illustrated in Extracts 3.8 and 3.9, but based on the corpus of all the children's talk in the 12 classes in which we recorded) helps us understand how children's interthinking goes well and how it goes badly. Our discussion of the two extracts we have presented illustrates several general issues about the development of children's skills in interthinking, and the use of digital technology to support their activity, which we will now discuss in more detail.

Collaboration, talk and learning

We mentioned in Chapter 1 that although the evidence is clear that collaborative activity is extremely useful for helping students study a range of subjects, including science, mathematics and literature, researchers have also frequently reported that in most classrooms group work is often not very productive. They report that children often do not share their knowledge effectively, some group members do not participate while others dominate and they interact in a quarrelsome, disputational manner (see Slavin 2009, Littleton and Howe 2010 and Mercer and Littleton 2007 for discussions of such research). It seems that many children, perhaps most, have not learned how to use talk well for managing their collaborations and reasoning together; yet the development of such skills is rarely made part of the curriculum, and few children are provided with guidance on how to carry out group work by their teachers. All available evidence indicates that the incidence of Exploratory Talk is low in classrooms across the world, even though – as we have seen in earlier chapters – this is the kind of talk that is most productive for problem-solving and collaborative learning.

As we have mentioned earlier in the book, our own research (as reported in Mercer and Littleton 2007) and that of others (Rojas-Drummond, Pérez, Vélez, Gómez & Mendoza 2003; Webb & Mastergeorge 2003; Reznitskaya *et al.* 2006) has shown that children can be helped to recognize the value of Exploratory Talk and to use it when appropriate. If teachers model the kinds of discussion they hope children will engage in and get the children to agree a set of suitable ground rules for regulating their group activity and generating Exploratory Talk, the quality of their group work can be transformed. As we explained in Chapter 1, such ground rules represent an *intermental* regulatory framework that is a template for the children's *intramental* co-regulation of their joint activity.

With the aim of maximizing the occurrence of Exploratory Talk, the teachers in our IWB project used the resources provided in the books of one of our colleagues, Lyn Dawes, (Dawes 2010, 2011) to establish suitable ground rules for talk with their classes, emphasizing principles such as

- all relevant information is shared;
- all members of the group are invited to contribute to the discussion;
- opinions and ideas are respected and considered;
- everyone is asked to give their reasons for their views;
- challenges and alternatives are made explicit and negotiated;
- the group seeks to reach agreement before taking a decision or acting.

The teachers had also been provided with examples of activities for developing children's talk awareness and skills, which suggested that they

> Ask groups to think together using 'What do you think?' and 'Why do you think that?' Stress the importance of asking for and giving reasons . . .
>
> *(Dawes 2010: 93)*

In all the classes involved, the idea of ground rules was introduced for the first time during this project. Extracts 4.3–4.8 show different groups of children in the project classes talking together. We have italicized some phrases that we think indicate their understanding of the use of ground rules for reasoning together and co-regulating joint activity in the group. The forms of language used by the children – 'What do . . . we all think?', 'Why do we think that?' echo the language used by their teacher in whole-class sessions, which in turn could be traced back to the guidance and activities in Lyn Dawes' books.

EXTRACT 4.3 Year 5: Class A – teeth
S1: But I don't, I doubt they'll have any canines, I doubt they have canines. I doubt that.
S2: *So what, so, so, do we all think* that they're not pointy?
S3: Yeah.

EXTRACT 4.4 Year 4: solids and liquids
S1: Vinegar is a liquid because like.
S2: It can go round couldn't it? Like if you get *(inaudible)*.
S1: Vinegar.
S2: *What's the reason though?*
S3: Water is because you can drink it.
S1: You can't uh; if you were drinking it you would be *(inaudible)*.

EXTRACT 4.5 Year 4: solids and liquids
S3: Rub soap, put it in the glass and then it forms into another one.
S2: So *that's the whole reason, yeah let's write that down.*
S1: You have to wet soap, a bar of soap. What about the other kind of soap? Bar of soap. Uh what did I say? Is a solid. Because?

EXTRACT 4.6 Year 5: reflective and non-reflective materials
S3: Shall we just put it in the middle?
S1: For now yeah. *Why do we think that?*

S1: Both. Because probably the light um, the glow worm the light bit, is probably um boun – the light from it bounces onto the um, the glow worm or something. Leave it Chloe OK?

S3: Right so, so right.

S1: *So why do we think those first? Why do we think those first?*

S2: I think the sun is definitely a light source.

EXTRACT 4.7 Year 5: reflective and non–reflective materials

S3: I think it should be fabric.

S1: Fabric.

S2: Fabric.

S3: So.

S2: What for a T–shirt?

S3: Yeah.

S2: *No don't, don't write anything yet because we haven't really discussed it.*

EXTRACT 4.8 Year 5: reflective and non–reflective materials

S3: So it could be that one, that one, so blue.

S1: So let's circle the first one. So we want um, or just choose first.

S1: What are you going to write Rita? *We need to say why as well.*

(Adapted from Warwick, Mercer & Kershner 2013)

Explicit references to reasoning, as represented by the italicized phrases, are rare in ordinary conversations among primary school children. Their incidence here, as they are used to co-regulate the discussion, can therefore be taken as indicative of the beginning of a transfer of responsibility for the quality of talk from teacher to students. Although this co-regulatory and exploratory way of talking in groups may not yet have been fully internalized by the children, we can see that they are using relevant common knowledge about how to do so.

Children's initial invocation of the ground rules and principles of Exploratory Talk, as in the examples above, may represent a transition phase, during which the responsibility for co-regulation is transferred from a teacher to the group. For some children, this process seemed well under way in a very short time. In classes where the teachers made talk a consistent focus, children used the ground rules with apparent ease, expressing reasoning, asking questions and striving towards agreement without articulating these things as specific intentions within their group activity. The rules had apparently provided scaffolding for their activity that was initially quite explicit and prescriptive but faded over time. The transfer of responsibility for engaging in Exploratory Talk can thus be seen to progress through three phases – teacher responsibility, joint responsibility and student responsibility. The final stage is illustrated by Extract 4.9, in which children were engaging freely in Exploratory Talk at appropriate points in their dialogues (the features of such talk are italicized in this example).

EXTRACT 4.9 Year 5: food chains

S2: *What do you think* would eat the tree?
S3: Um, *maybe* the caterpillar might eat the tree?
S2: Not eat the whole tree.
S1: Well eat the plants.
S3: Yeah it'll eat the leaves.
S1: Wait *lets just think about this*. Let's see, that *could* go in there, and um then that, but that *could* be.
S3: *Maybe* the Mayfly could eat the leaves off the?
S2: *I don't think* (inaudible).
S1: No, no, no actually. Put this in there.
(One pupil removes the oak tree and replaces it with the algae)
S2: Algae.
S1: Then Mayfly, oh no back. Then *maybe* that could go on there yeah?
S3: Yeah.
S2: Oh what about the frog?

(Adapted from Warwick, Mercer & Kershner 2013)

Extract 4.9 illustrates one further interesting feature of the children's talk – that ideas can be expressed through a combination of dialogue and the use of the IWB; for example, when S1 above says 'Let's see, that *could* go in there, and um then that, but that *could* be' they are representing their ideas not simply by speaking but by moving objects to provisional positions on the IWB.

As part of the sociocultural discourse analysis we carried out for this study, our initial qualitative examination of children's talk was complemented by a quantitative analysis of the recorded talk. As described in Chapter 2, this involved the use of concordance software for locating and quantifying the incidence of relevant words or expressions in the transcribed talk. The analysis generated by concordance software such as MonoConc (which was used in this research) or Wordsmith not only register the relative occurrence of any items targeted, but enable a researcher to identify easily the linguistic context in which they were spoken (by presenting each incidence of a term embedded in the relevant part of the transcript). This permits the researcher to check on the apparent meaning of the term in context. This is important because within sociocultural discourse analysis the quantitative method is not meant be used independently from the qualitative analysis. For example, in an earlier study (Mercer *et al.* 2004) a combination of qualitative and quantitative analysis showed that relative higher incidence of certain key items – 'because', 'I think', 'would' and 'could' – was associated with children's increased use of Exploratory Talk.

In this study of children's use of the IWB, one of the aims of our concordance analysis was to assess the relative extent to which items that the qualitative analysis showed were associated with Exploratory Talk were found in the talk of children in the classes of different teachers. Table 4.1 provides a summary of that analysis for classes recorded in the classrooms of four participating teachers (H, C, S and P) at approximately the same time in the project. The contributions of children in all parts of the recorded lesson (whole class discussions as well as the recorded group sessions) are included. As well as the items associated with Exploratory Talk, the table also includes the relative incidence of the use of 'we' by the children, because our qualitative analysis suggested its use was associated with children's reference to collective activity and the invocation of common goals and imperatives.

It can be seen that the relative incidence of the terms varies across the four classes. Using the total incidence of these terms per class as an index of the extent of Exploratory Talk and an orientation to the pursuit of common goals, it would seem that the children in the classes of teachers H and C generated most talk of that kind, with those in S and P's classes generating it least. Not quite all the variation among the classes is in the

TABLE 4.1 Example of concordance analysis; relative incidence of key words in the talk of children in one recorded lesson in four classrooms (Adapted from Warwick *et al.* 2013)

	Teacher H	*Teacher C*	*Teacher S*	*Teacher P*
Because	94	101	23	21
Agree(d/s)	4	4	2	0
Could/Would/Should	47	19	10	8
If	28	25	6	13
Why	1	13	6	10
Think	56	54	19	18
Couldn't	0	1	0	0
Wouldn't	4	3	0	0
Shouldn't	0	0	0	1
Explain	7	1	0	1
We ('re/'ll/'d/'ve)	196	81	43	31

expected direction, with the relative incidence of 'why' being anomalous, but this quantitative analysis supported the conclusion we had drawn from the qualitative analysis: that teacher H had provided the strongest and clearer guidance to children about using suitable 'ground rules' for talking together and regulating group activity, and that teacher P had provided the least.

Improvable objects and interthinking

As we saw earlier, the IWB is very useful for generating and recording synoptic, written conclusions; it is easy for the whole group to see and comment on what each member writes, and for the final text to be very quickly modified in light of feedback and evaluation of the emerging ideas (see Littleton, Twiner and Gillen 2010). One of our former doctoral students, Alison Twiner, has called the kind of text the children are creating on the IWB a 'digital improvable object' (Twiner 2011; Twiner, Littleton, Coffin & Whitelock in press). Teachers often encourage children to record what has been said in their group discussions. It was the classroom researcher Gordon Wells (1999) who first suggested that if they are treated as 'improvable objects' rather than finished pieces of work, such records can, if used appropriately, provide a cumulative basis of common knowledge upon which future discussions and other activities can draw and progressively build. Of course, such records do not have to be digital – they can also be created on paper – but computer-based technology offers a way of doing so easily, so that modifications can be made, several versions kept and copies distributed. Such digital records can also include other things such as diagrams and drawings that capture ideas created in discussions. They can offer a kind of half-way stage between the ephemerality of talk and the permanence of written texts, and represent one way that technology can help people think collectively. However, we should recall that the children in Extract 4.2 seemed to treat their digital notes on the IWB as a kind of finalized, public presentation, rather than an informal resource for future group activity. The affordances of technology will only be emerge if they are in accord with the relevant social norms.

An example of an improvable object, of a multimodal kind, is reproduced below, taken from a project in which a series of Personal, Social and Health Education lessons were recorded (Littleton, Twiner & Gillen 2010). During one lesson in which the children were exploring and discussing issues concerned with peer-group dynamics and peer pressure, the teacher had chosen a DVD extract of a televised drama to show the class. After getting the pupils to watch it through once in full, the teacher began replaying the DVD – pausing it at key points to encourage the pupils to discuss the motives, intentions and feelings of the characters in the drama. At each of these points, when the image was frozen on-screen, she invited students to annotate the image by using the IWB pen to write their comments and reactions on the IWB (see Figure 4.2). In this instance, the frozen frame was of a character's face, and pupils had been asked to suggest words to describe how that particular character might be feeling at that moment. Having captured multiple suggestions the annotated frozen still and associated annotations were captured and saved as a screen grab. This summarized the students' key ideas and reactions at that point in the lesson.

As the students were making their suggestions and adding their annotations, the teacher linked them to the aims and content of the curriculum. Once saved, this collective creation was then available as a tangible resource for discussion by groups of students. For example, the teacher reloaded it onto the whiteboard screen for them to refer to when considering the changing feelings of the character as events in the drama unfolded. It was both a powerful *aide memoire* for initial reactions and ideas and a subsequent focus for collective thinking.

FIGURE 4.2 A pupil annotating the frozen DVD image.

Other kinds of electronic text can also support the collective revision, development and evaluation of ideas. For example, one of us (KL) has been involved in the development of software that enables secondary school students to design and run their own science inquiries at school, at home, or outdoors on mobile devices (http://www.nquire.org.uk). Within this software, comment boxes enable groups of students to capture, during the data collection phase of their inquiries, important contextual information that would assist them in the interpretation of the data during analysis. Observations of the software in use revealed that as the students moved towards the reporting of their investigation, they also reworked, refined and continually edited and saved the text within the boxes. In doing so the text became an ongoing work in progress, capturing emerging ideas and (inter)thinking, over time, in respect of the interpretation of data and key findings. Their initial comments recorded in the boxes provided a base from which to develop and build shared knowledge and understanding. This process of reworking the comments in the boxes also helped students make connections across different phases of the inquiry and so help them maintain the 'thread' of their joint activity (see Littleton and Kerawalla 2010 for more information).

As with any computer-based technology, we have noticed that technical failures or inscrutable responses by machines sometimes stop children's activity altogether, leaving them adrift while they wait for help from the teacher. We are not uncritical advocates of the use of technology in education, and recognize its limitations. Nevertheless, the use of IWBs illustrates well how computers and other cultural tools can resource face-to-face talk and thereby enable interthinking. As a tool for enabling interthinking by a group, 'tabletop' interactive computers that are sensitive to touch may prove to be more useful. At the time of writing, their use by groups of children in UK primary schools is being explored by Steve Higgins and his colleagues at Durham (Higgins, Mercier, Burd & Hatch 2011). Another researcher, Stahl (2011), has suggested that tabletops could serve as a 'multimedia tribal fire for the classroom, workplace, or social gathering', though they are currently so costly that it is unlikely that they will soon become as common in classrooms as the IWB.

Collaborative learning and prescriptive tutoring

We will now describe some research carried out by another of our research students, Benson Soong, for his doctoral project (Soong & Mercer 2011). This study represents a kind of bridge between the face-to-face inter-actions of a conventional classroom and collaborative learning in an online environment. The research was based in a secondary school in Singapore, and involved a class of 15-year-olds at a point when they were revising for their General Certificate of Education in physics. Their teacher, Siew Shin Er, was actively involved throughout (Soong, Mercer & Siew 2010).

The usual way of helping students prepare for these examinations in this school was to provide them with worksheets of the kinds of problems they would be likely to encounter and ask them to work on them individually, or in pairs, in the classroom. They could of course ask the teacher for help, if and when they thought they needed it. In this research situation, the students were each given access to a machine in the school's computer laboratory. Worksheets were then handed out and, using Microsoft NetMeeting, each student was then paired up online with another member of their class (not chosen, or identified, by them). They were asked to try to solve the problems in the worksheets collaboratively with their anonymous partner, using only online communication through NetMeeting and its whiteboard facility.

Prior to the first computer lab session, it was explained to the students why they were being asked to use computers to solve the physics problems with an anonymous partner. They were also asked to agree to follow a set of ground rules designed to encourage online communication resembling Exploratory Talk (see Figure 4.3).

During the computer lab session (which lasted an hour or a little longer), the students were required to regularly save both their shared text-chat and whiteboard comments onto a shared virtual directory, which the researcher and teacher could access at the end of each session and use for analysis. The students had agreed that their teacher could have full access to all the logs of the discussions. After every session, the students completed a very short survey about their participation.

Extract 4.10 comes from the discussion of two students (who nicknamed themselves Qwerty and Yayi) as they attempted to solve the following problem: 'A beaker of water at room temperature was placed under a sealed bell jar. The air pump is turned on. State whether you agree with the following statements.' The worksheet then listed a series of statements, the first of which was 'The temperature of the water falls'. In Extract 4.10, Qwerty and Yayi are considering this statement. (The words in square brackets ([. . .]) are the researchers' interpretative comments on what the students are doing.)

EXTRACT 4.10 Why does the temperature of water fall?
Qwerty: part 1 reason:
Yayi: is cold because less air molecule

[Yayi seems to be suggesting that the temperature of the water in the beaker falls as a result of there being fewer air molecules in the jar]

Qwerty: when the air molecules are being sucked up

Qwerty: less molecules are colliding with the water surface

Qwerty: hence temperature drops

[Here, we see that while Qwerty reached the correct answer, his explanation is incorrect]

Yayi: ya

[By agreeing with Qwerty, Yayi also reveals her own misconceptions on what caused the temperature of the water to fall]

(*Adapted from Soong, Mercer & Siew 2010*)

The students had recently had a lesson on heat, temperature and the kinetic theory of matter. In the opinion of their teacher, they should have been aware that the decrease in temperature of the water in the beaker was associated with the slower motion of the water molecules. However, as evident from their discussion, both Qwerty and Yayi believed that the decrease in temperature of the water in the beaker was the result of fewer collisions in the jar between air molecules and water molecules. In other words, they seemed to believe that temperature is directly related to

---

Ground Rules

A key objective of getting you to work with a partner through the computer is so that we may see your thought processes when your team is solving the questions that we posed. When we have insights into your thought processes, we would be able to uncover your physics misconceptions or misunderstandings, thereby allowing us to specifically target your weaker areas. Hence, it is important that you have a good working relationship with your partner. To help you establish a good working relationship with your partner, here are the ground rules.

The basic ground rules for "chatting" online are:

- You agree to share your ideas and listen to each other, no matter how silly it might appear.
- You agree to consider what your partner has written or drawn.
- You agree to respect each other's opinions.
- You agree to give reasons for your ideas.
- You agree to express your ideas and workings neatly and clearly.
- If you disagree, you will ask "why?" or provide reasons for your disagreement.
- You agree not to discuss any topic that is not related to physics, including asking your partner who he/she is.
- You agree to only work on solving the problems (e.g. no web-surfing!).
- You and your partner must agree on a solution prior to asking the teacher to check the answer.

FIGURE 4.3 The ground rules students were required to follow during the computer laboratory sessions.

collisions between molecules, not the relative speed of molecules. In the case of the problem posed, since there would be fewer air molecules in the beaker once the air pump was switched on, Qwerty reasoned that this reduced collisions between air molecules and the water molecules, causing the water temperature to fall. This reasoning is incorrect and not consistent with what they had recently been taught. From the logs of their discussions, the teacher and researchers could see that more than half of the students in this physics class shared this misconception.

Reviewing the students' discussion logs, it seemed clear that many of the pairs benefited from revising collaboratively, and that they used an online version of Exploratory Talk to do so. Their own reflections were generally positive, making comments afterwards in the survey such as 'It is a good change to study together and learn from each other' and 'Very fun!' But the logs of their discussions also enabled the teacher to take account of the misunderstandings they demonstrated as the basis for whole-class revision sessions, rather than using a pre-specified lesson plan. In other words, subsequent lessons became opportunities for a kind of contingent teaching that Soong has called 'prescriptive tutoring'.

This combination of online collaborative learning and prescriptive tutoring was evaluated by assessing the learning gains of the 21 students in the class. Using a pretest/post-test design, a pre-test was conducted for the entire class prior to the conduct of the intervention. Thereafter, one set of seven students served as a control group (following the usual procedures for revision sessions), another set of seven who attended after-school tuition physics lessons were designated as an alternate intervention group (as they were receiving a different kind of additional help with their revision), while the remaining seven students served as the experimental group (who worked together online and were encouraged to use the ground rules for Exploratory Talk). Statistical comparisons showed that students in the experimental group obtained significantly higher post-test scores – an improvement of more than 25 per cent – than students in the control or alternate intervention groups.

Collaborative learning at a distance

The Open University has been a leading developer of online courses and resources for distance education, and as colleagues there we both experienced the shift over time from a reliance on printed and broadcast materials, supplemented by occasional face-to-face meetings, to a substantial reliance on digital resources and computer-based communications. There have been many studies of the use of electronic communications in distance education, but few have been studies of how spoken or written communication between students in distant locations might enable their learning or problem-solving. However, the findings of such research as there is can help us infer what constitutes effective communication in virtual educational environments, what problems arise and how they can be resolved.

One of the ways that communicating through text online is rather different from talking face-to-face is that it can either take place in real time, so that speakers respond immediately to each other, or people may take some time to respond. An online 'conversation' can be spread out over a period of days, weeks or even months. Ingram and Hathorn, two researchers into the uses of online communication in education, describe the differences between these two modes of computer-mediated communication (CMC) as follows:

> CMC can be divided into synchronous and asynchronous modes. In synchronous communications all participants are online at the same time, while asynchronous communications occurs without time constraints. Synchronous discussion involves the use of programs, such as chat rooms, instant messengers or audio and video programs, in which all participants exchange messages in real time. Messages appear on the screen almost immediately after they are typed, and many threads can occur simultaneously. Those who have experienced these rapid exchanges of information, ideas, and opinions know that even extraordinary typing skill and quick response times do not guarantee that one can keep up with the constantly changing discussion. Hence, synchronous discussion may be best suited for brainstorming and quickly sharing ideas. In asynchronous discussions students can participate at any time and from any location, without regard to what other discussants are doing. Asynchronous CMC allows participants to contribute to the discussion more equally because none of the customary limitations imposed by an instructor or class schedule apply. Full and free expression of ideas is possible. Although these communications are text-based, they have little in common with traditional printed information. Experienced users use a style that is characterized by abbreviated writing and emoticons (e.g., smileys). Asynchronous discussions, which can occur over e-mail or threaded Web discussion, allow more time for considered opinions ... and are more effective for deeper discussion of ideas.
>
> *(Ingram & Hathorn 2004: 220)*

On its inception, online communication was widely expected to generate new styles of learning, because students would be able engage with their studies at times and in locations that suited them best rather than being constrained by conventional timetables of attendance. Enthusiasts for online distance education generally saw this as a positive shift. However, enthusiasts for radical changes in education often overlook the ways that some of the needs of students may be being met successfully by more traditional methods, and how new modes of communication might not serve those needs as well. Moreover, students have their own views about how best to learn. This is not only an issue with the use of CMC, as two researchers into online education comment:

> At a regional educational conference several years ago, two participants were observed walking out during the introduction of a concurrent session. After introducing the topic, the presenter asked participants to form into small groups for further work. Obviously distraught over this methodological turn in the session, one turned to the other and said, "Don't they just lecture anymore? I get so sick of this group stuff." This comment reveals the profound ambivalence that many learners feel towards collaborative learning methods in general and group work, in particular. While learners often express a desire to be more engaged and active in their learning, they are often less than enthusiastic about learning through small group work. Online technologies often exacerbate learners' ambivalence toward group work.
>
> *(Dirkx & Smith 2004: 132–133)*

They also report this comment from one university student who had been involved in an online collaborative learning course, as illustrating how the lack of more conventional opportunities for interthinking can be a problem:

> Right now we're getting down to trying to finalize our final problem, and it's hard to get everybody's thoughts and feelings into this paper — just communicating over the computer. Where if we were in a group together, it would be a lot easier to exchange ideas and information, as opposed to over the computer, where you have to always type everything. It's hard to refer back to something else and see what's going on.
>
> *(Dirkx & Smith 2004: 149)*

The challenges that distance education students often experience in using CMC have been well documented by Open University colleagues and others (Mason 1995; Morris & Naughton 1999; Tolmie & Boyle 2000). Nevertheless, many students appreciate the flexibility of time and location that online communication allows. As with group work, students may come to appreciate its value once they have experienced it and if they are given suitable guidance in how to make the most of it. Distance educators need to make the best use of the affordances of digital technology so as to compensate for the loss of some of the most attractive and useful features of more traditional ways of teaching and learning.

At the Open University, Rebecca Ferguson, who carried out her doctoral research with one of us (KL), investigated just these kinds of issues (Ferguson 2009; Ferguson, Whitelock & Littleton 2010). She was interested in how students working online managed the task of building knowledge and understanding together, as they pursued assignments in groups. The students involved mainly used asynchronous communication, through a medium called First Class, but they could communicate synchronously if they wished. Her data came from six week-long online conferences in which small groups of undergraduate psychology students developed and carried out research projects. At the end of these periods of collaboration, each group presented their work to the other people on the course and received feedback from fellow students. This was intended to help them complete their subsequent coursework. Their participation in the group work was assessed; students could not pass the course without being judged as taking an active role within their group.

One of Ferguson's initial hypotheses was that the three kinds of talk that we had observed children using in classroom group work – Disputational, Cumulative and Exploratory Talk, as described in Chapter 1 – might also be observed in the online, asynchronous discussion of these students. She therefore analyzed all the posts related to the joint task made by members of three groups of students, over the period they worked together. She did this by using an adapted version of our own approach to analyzing talk in classrooms, Sociocultural Discourse Analysis (Mercer 2004; Mercer, Littleton & Wegerif 2004), as also described in Chapter 1. However, she quite rightly noted that a limitation of this method of analysis is that it does not deal with visual elements of communication, except by making references to them in notes accompanying transcriptions. The asynchronous dialogue of the online conferences she studied had both verbal and visual elements, with much of the meaning carried by diagrams, tables and other visual features such as layout and typography. As the linguists Kress and van Leeuwen (1996) have argued, to understand how participants construct meanings together, discussions involving such objects need to be analyzed as an integrated whole, as multimodal texts. These ideas drew Ferguson's attention to occasions when the students relied particularly heavily on additional resources, which could not only be graphic items but also other kinds of linguistic texts, such as transcripts of the talk of children recorded as part of their research. Some

<u>**Consolidation of om analysis**</u>

To make it easier I have coloured coded our results, and put our names in front of it. Charlene, Ethan, Andrea, Rita.

<u>Lines we all commented on our comments.</u>

15

Charlene: The Doctor is very patronising and casting doubt in the confidence of the patient straight away, by saying that he guesses the patient doesn't remember too much about what he has told him.

Ethan: Doctor's tone indicates a slight disinterest in the notes and desire to move onto finding out information from the patient about what he remembers of the procedure. He also assumes the patient does not remember a lot. He is making a negative assumption about the patient, which may be interpreted as a desire to be seen as the knowledgeable party. This could be seen as an attempt at power.

Andrea: The doctor in a show of confidence and authority makes direct eye contact with the patient and tells him in a patronising way (as if to imply he would not be able to remember what he had previously been told in earlier conversations) about what he had been told before.

Rita: The use at times of almost childish language by the doctor looks to be belittling of the patient and the communication of the patient becomes more and more quiet, with only softly spoken, (yeah) which becomes more prominent when the doctor talks about the possible consequences of the operation.

FIGURE 4.4 Start of 15-page consolidation document posted by Charlene on 16 December (Adapted from Ferguson 2009: 254).

were very obviously improvable objects, as discussed earlier in the chapter, such as documents generated by one or more students that summarized what the group had achieved together in their work so far and that members of the group could add to or modify as their work progressed. She called these distinctive episodes of interaction that were heavily mediated by such objects *attached dialogue*. An example from her data of an object that functioned in this way – a summary of analytic comments made by group members, prepared by one student – is shown in Figure 4.4.

Ferguson also usefully identified some important ways that asynchronous online interactions among a group are different from those among people working face-to-face, in terms of the resources group members have to support their interthinking. For example, they often have digital improvable objects of the kind that we mentioned earlier. As she comments:

They do not need to employ devices that will help them to remember what they have said or done, because they have access to the complete text of their past dialogue in a transcript automatically generated by the software. What they need to replace is the range of tones, expressions and gestures available to support sense making in a face-to-face setting. They must find asynchronous methods of agreeing on what they have achieved together, and on how they can shape past dialogue to build shared knowledge. At the same time, they need to avoid disagreements and find a way of moving dialogue forward safely when only a subset of the group is online and able to participate.

(Ferguson op. cit.: 168)

The temporally extended, and even disjointed nature of online talk creates different kinds of obstacles to interthinking from face-to-face settings. Requests for explanations and checks of understanding are more laborious to make, as are the responses they require; and so any disagreements that arise are harder, to resolve. Ferguson did not observe much 'flaming' behaviour online or other uncooperative exchanges that would have represented an online version of Disputational Talk, but these were reported in interviews by students and tutors. She also noted that the unsynchronized manner in which students join and leave continuing online conferences can also pose a problem, because a student could waste time pursuing a line of thought that then turned out to be irrelevant or redundant because the online dialogue had taken an unexpected turn after they had logged out. This is reflected in the experience of one of the students involved in her study who did not have daily access to the conference in which he was working. He reported that his group:

initially decided to select articles from four randomly selected newspapers over a three day period, 26th–28th, of November. As I am living in Greece I could buy the aforementioned newspapers with one day delay. By the time I had bought the first series of the newspapers some members of the group did not bothered [sic] to buy the rest of the papers and decided not to continue with that article collection.

(Ferguson op. cit.: 167)

As in other research on Open University students' online interactions (Wegerif 1998; Littleton & Whitelock 2005), Ferguson found that most of the communication among group members resembled Cumulative Talk: relevant information was shared and there was little dispute or display of negative emotions, but there was also little reasoned argument and few attempts to use questions to find out more about what any member of the group thought. In other words, there was relatively little of the online equivalent of Exploratory Talk – though, as mentioned earlier, there was also very little resembling Disputational Talk. However, when she looked in detail at the episodes of attached dialogue, she found there were more 'exploratory' features such as reasons, challenges, questions and so on. Such discussion also often led to group members resorting to synchronous discussion online (that is, communicating electronically in real time) in order to sort things out. These strategies, of employing improvable objects to support their discussions, and resorting to synchronous talk when it seemed beneficial, seemed to enable groups to achieve successful outcomes for their learning tasks. When students adapted their ways of communicating to suit the affordances of the medium in which they were working and – crucially – they engaged at appropriate times in a kind of discussion that resembled Exploratory Talk, they were able to interthink very effectively online.

Other research involving higher education students working together online is also helpful for understanding what makes interthinking effective in virtual environments. For example, note this conclusion drawn by two researchers whose work we mentioned earlier:

> Consensus is critical to the process [of working successfully together online] because it is only through consensus that the members of the group are required to listen, hear, understand and finally accept the view point of fellow group members. When students are forced, through dialogue and deliberation, to come to consensus, they must work harder to consider all viewpoints, in order to reach agreement
> *(Dirkx & Smith 2004: 137)*

There are some interesting links to be made here with research our Cambridge colleague Christine Howe (2010) has reported, on a series of studies on collaborative learning in science in Scottish primary schools. The children were given various kinds of enquiry activities. For example, in one activity pairs of eight-year-olds were asked to predict whether an empty metal box or a solid rubber ring would float in a tank of water. Having made a prediction, they would then test this with real objects. In one set of classes, children were asked by their teachers to try to reach an agreement within their group about their predictions, before they carried out the tests. In another set of classes, they were simply asked to work together on the tasks. After a substantial delay of some weeks, members of each class were tested on their understanding of the relevant phenomena. It was found that children obtained significantly better results on these delayed tests of learning and understanding when they were asked to seek agreement on their predictions before testing them. Moreover, it did not seem to matter whether agreement was actually reached, or if contrasting views were reconciled. What was important was that seeking agreement was a feature of their group discussions. In explaining these results, Howe suggests that having to seek agreement encourages children to pursue their discussions in more depth and to more certain conclusions. Conflict between their ideas during conversation primes children's metacognition – their reflections about their own thinking – with the result that they subsequently give more consideration to what they think about the phenomenon, and to the significance of their observations. This is in accord with the results of other studies involving adult participants, which found that the generation of debate was a requirement for group activities to lead to improved performance on reasoning tasks: see, for example, Schulz-Hardt, Brodbeck, Mojzisch, Kerschreiter and Frey (2006). It is therefore tempting to draw some generalizations about what makes interthinking successful, whether it involves children or adults, and whether it happens face-to-face or online.

The researchers Ingram and Hathorn have also offered some useful insights into the communications of students working together online. They make the same kind of distinction between 'cooperative' and 'collaborative' learning that we noted Moran and John-Steiner (2004) and Seddon (2004) making in Chapter 3:

> Cooperation is defined as the style of working, sometimes called "divide-and-conquer," in which students split an assignment into roughly equal pieces to be completed by the individuals, and then stitched together to finish the assignment.
>
> In contrast, we define collaboration as a more complex working together. Students discuss all parts of the assignment, adding and changing things in conjunction with one another as they come to understand more about the topic.
>
> At the end, the final product is truly a group product in which it is difficult or impossible to identify individual contributions. There appear to be differences between cooperation and collaboration in both the complexity of the interactions and the effectiveness for instruction and education.
>
> *(Ingram & Hathorn 2004: 216)*

On the basis of their analysis of groups of university students using asynchronous CMC to work together, they offer the following observations:

> One of the characteristics of the most collaborative group was the very low incidence of interaction with the instructor ... The group worked almost entirely independently. The only interaction with the instructor was a short reply to an instruction on chat procedures.

There was no instructor involvement in the actual discussion of the scenario.

In contrast, the instructor was a significant contributor to the total number of messages in the least collaborative group, contributing the second most messages in the group ... Although instructor messages were shorter the instructor nevertheless contributed the second highest number of statements in that group.

(Ingram & Hathorn 2004: 238)

Concluding remarks

We have shown that the use of various kinds of digital tools, whether an IWB by groups of children in a classroom or an asynchronous CMC environment by university students at a distance, can provide some valuable support for productive discussion. They can resource what Wegerif (2007, 2010) has called a 'dialogic space' in which different ideas, perspectives and understandings can be collectively explored, and material can be modified to record the development of a discussion and capture emerging ideas. Digital communication offers opportunities for students to interthink online, and to do so without the constraints of time and location that arise in more conventional educational settings. However, we have also noted that any technology has its own limitations, and new modes of communication may not provide some of the same kinds of support for interthinking as more traditional methods.

The conclusion we draw from research on online communication is that similar kinds of expectations should apply to members of virtual groups as have been found to apply to face-to-face groups, if collaborative learning is to be most successfully pursued. Users still need to learn effective ways of interthinking. More than one way of talking can be productive but discussion is likely to be most productive for learning if participants agree to follow the kinds of ground rules for discussion that will generate an online version of Exploratory Talk. Therefore, they should be expected to encourage universal participation among group members, seek ideas and clarification of them, challenge ideas and proposals in respectful ways if they have good reason to do so and support their own ideas and proposals with reasons and explanations. As in conventional group work, Cumulative Talk can also have a useful function at certain points in joint learning activity, for example to gather all possibly relevant ideas for consideration or report. However, it seems unlikely that Disputational Talk is any more useful or productive online than it is face-to-face.

5

LANGUAGE AND THE PROCESS OF THINKING COLLECTIVELY

Introduction

In this chapter we will consolidate what is currently known about the process of interthinking, drawing on the ideas and research findings we have discussed in previous chapters. Essentially, we aim to provide a sociocultural account of the process, of the kind we outlined in Chapter 1, which acknowledges the relationship between individual thinking and collective thinking, the cultural and social contexts in which people think collectively and the prime role that language plays in linking human minds. In the first part of the chapter, we will use the findings of educational research on classroom talk and psychological studies of the development of children's thinking and communication skills to discuss how people learn to interthink and how individual thinking is related to collective thinking. Using the concepts we have discussed, we then offer an explanation of how and why collective thinking can be successful among people of any age, and relate that explanation to the various domains of activity we have discussed in the previous chapters.

Towards the end of the chapter, we return to a topic we considered in Chapter 3, creativity as a collective achievement, and relate this to a sociocultural account of interthinking and its development. Finally, we set out some of the key concepts we have introduced, and draw some general conclusions.

The development of individual and collective thinking

Many educational researchers have investigated the processes of collaborative learning, through studying how children of various ages work together in groups on set tasks and assessing the outcomes. The main aim of such research has typically been to ascertain if working in groups without a teacher is a good way of helping individual students learn and improve their understanding. Likewise, psychological research on young children's collective play activities has been mainly concerned with understanding the influence of social interaction on the ways individuals come to think and learn. That is, although concerned with collaborative activity, such research has had, at basis, an individualistic focus. It has not been intended to provide a better explanation of how people learn to solve problems and make sense of the world together. Nevertheless, as we will explain, its findings can help us understand the processes of interthinking in general, if we bring it together with the findings of research in other areas of enquiry.

Most of our own research has been applied educational research. It has been motivated by the aim of helping teachers make the most of opportunities for talk, in both whole class and small group settings; with enabling children to use talk effectively for learning and problem-solving; and with understanding how talk can develop children's reasoning capabilities. The series of school-based research projects we carried out with Rupert Wegerif, Lyn Dawes, Sylvia Rojas-Drummond and other colleagues (usually known as the *Thinking Together* research) was described in detail in our previous book, *Dialogue and the Development of Children's Thinking* (Mercer & Littleton 2007). We will draw on what was found in that research, but we will not duplicate that information here. We will not give much attention either to how children can be taught to use language to interthink, because we and our colleagues have written extensively about that elsewhere (see, for example, Dawes 2008, 2010, 2011, 2013; Littleton and Howe 2010; Mercer 1995; Mercer and Hodgkinson 2008; Littleton and Mercer 2013; Wegerif and Dawes 2005). Instead, we will consider what that research can tell us about the development of children's ability to think collectively, and how it might inform our understanding of interthinking in general.

The talk environment of children's lives

Our main concern in this book is with people of a similar age and status working and thinking together – what might be called 'symmetrical' interactions, rather than the more 'asymmetrical' interactions in which a parent or teacher instructs or guides learners through an activity. The foundations of children's ability to use language to think, collectively and alone, can be found in the conversations they have with adults. There is considerable variation in the amount and quality of talk that pre-school children are involved in at home, and it has been known for some time that children's success in school during their teenage years can be linked to their early language experiences (Hart & Risley 1995). It has also been shown that conversations with parents and others in the home can assist children's literacy development and their ability to remember events, with the children of parents who involve them in 'elaborative' conversations performing best (Fivush & Hammond 1990; Reese, Haden & Fivush 1993; Wells 2009; Goswami & Bryant 2007). This is relevant to our interests here because elaborative conversations are essentially those in which a parent or other adult sets up a dialogue with a child about the situation in which they find themselves, and the pair use talk to think together about what is going on. Although typically led by one partner, the adult, elaborative conversations have some affinity with both Cumulative and Exploratory Talk in the way that ideas are shared openly and possible explanations for observed phenomena can be considered critically but in an atmosphere of trust. They can also reveal some interesting differences in perspective between adults and young children. Here is one such conversation our colleague Lyn Dawes recorded when a child we will call Rita (aged four) was with her childminder (Natalie) by the river, feeding the ducks.

EXTRACT 5.1 Feeding the ducks

Natalie: Lots of ducks. What do you think they are covered in, Rita?

Rita: Silk.

Natalie: Silk – hmm – how do you think they float?

Rita: They swim (*watching the ducks*) but in the water you can only see their back legs.

Natalie: Back legs? How many legs do they have?

Rita: Four.

Natalie: Well! Only two really. They've turned their front legs into wings I think.

Rita: (*In amused disbelief*) Hah!

Of course, the talk environment of a young child's home life cannot be explained only in terms of the conversational styles their parents or other carers have chosen to adopt. Nevertheless, because research evidence encourages the view that the amount and quality of conversation children are engaged in during their early years can have a significant impact on their intellectual development and educational attainment, some explanation of the role of language in that process is called for. A greater amount of children's involvement in talk at home may help them acquire larger vocabularies, and gain more information through talk from adults, but those factors do not seem a sufficient explanation in themselves. Although there is some association between the quality of talk in the home and socio-economic status, differences in attainment cannot be explained in terms of some children acquiring the kinds of accents and styles of talking associated with membership of the middle classes in many societies (however useful those may be for gaining social access to some echelons of society). Of course, many factors will affect an individual's educational attainment and social mobility; but, on the basis of available evidence, we suggest that the quality of early language experience is important because it is how children learn from those around them how to use language to make sense of the world and to *reason*.

Almost all children grow up in an environment that enables them to learn to speak, fluently, one or more languages. However, that does not mean that they will all have the same opportunities to learn a range of ways of using language to describe experience, manage social relationships, solve problems, argue their point of view and get things done. In Chapter 2, we discussed the kinds of specialized forms of language – *language genres* – that are associated with the pursuit of particular occupations or activities. Even within the parameters of ordinary, everyday life, we each need to learn a range of genres to get things done. Some are simple and very common genres that everyone is likely to learn, such as the exchange procedures used in buying something in a shop. Others, such as the genre of a 'reasoned discussion', are less common. Children learn these functional uses of language initially through becoming involved in interactions with older, more experienced members of our communities. Through the example and guidance of those older members of their community, children can learn how to provide clear explanations, to present reasoned arguments, to negotiate difficult emotional circumstances and so on. They can then employ and develop those skills when interacting with other children; this kind of practice will be vital for the development of their language skills.

There has been a great reluctance by many researchers of social language use and educational attainment, to accept that children of some families, or some communities, may have a language experience that is less 'rich' than that of others. A furore was provoked by the work of Basil Bernstein, back in the 1970s (Bernstein 1971, 1975), which linked the language habits of working class life with a 'restricted code' for making sense of the world, in which ideas and the reasons connecting them are rarely made explicit. This was contrasted with the 'elaborated code' said to typify language use of middle-class culture, and used to explain differential educational achievement between children of those different class backgrounds. Debate about Bernstein's theory of codes was very fierce and intense. It was claimed, with some justification, that his descriptions of the language styles of the middle and working classes were not based on solid empirical comparisons of language use in the lives of real families. One consequence was that any discussions of the codes, or any similar notions of some children experiencing a 'language deficit', became almost taboo among linguistic and educational researchers – even though alternative approaches did not provide a satisfactory explanation for differential educational achievement, and other well-grounded anthropological research illustrated well how differences between the language habits of different communities might be more or less well matched to the language of educational practice (for example Heath 1982).

In more recent years, however, research has generated a more nuanced version of the kind of account Bernstein offered. As the sociolinguist Gee puts it:

> School is, as it is presently constituted, ultimately all about learning specialist varieties of language, in particular academic varieties of language connected to content areas. Some children bring early prototypes of those academic varieties of language to school – prototypes they have learned at home. Some do not.
>
> *(Gee 2004: 19)*

Empirical research like that of Reese *et al.* (1993), Hart and Risley (1995) and Wells (2009), mentioned above, suggests that some links of the kind that Bernstein tried to make between communal ways of using language as a cultural tool and individual ways of using language as a cognitive tool deserve renewed consideration.

For some children, perhaps many, school may represent the only opportunity for experiencing and acquiring some valuable ways of using language as a means for thinking, both collectively and alone. Experience in providing explicit, clear explanations can be very useful in school, as can skills in reasoning about ideas and processes. 'Reasoned discussion' may be a genre that does not appear often in some children's out-of-school lives. From a sociocultural perspective, this is important because reasoning with other people provides children with a model for how to reason alone. For some children, educational success may be dependent on the extent to which school enables them to learn ways of using language as a tool for interthinking, as well as for thinking alone. This gives the quality of talk in classrooms a special significance.

Students' talk in groups

Studies of students in school working in groups – what is usually called 'collaborative learning' – have generated an interesting paradox. Collaborative work has been found to be a powerful aid to study, in all subjects including maths and science, and useful too for the development of 'transferable' reasoning and communication skills (see Slavin 2009; Howe 2010; Vass and Littleton 2010). However, research has also shown that in most classrooms, much of the time, group work is quite unproductive (see Littleton and Howe 2010). As we mentioned in Chapter 1, our own observations in school uphold this paradox. The solution to this paradox is that many students, perhaps most, do not know how to talk and work together effectively, but teachers assume that they do. They need to be taught how to do so; just giving them opportunities to collaborate is not enough. If they are taught how to use language to interthink, their collaborative activity becomes much more productive. Our own school-based studies, and those of others, have provided support for this argument. Research has shown that if teachers establish and maintain educationally productive dialogues with their students they can influence the ways students talk and work together in groups (see, for example, Webb, Nemer and Ing 2006; Webb 2009; Littleton and Howe 2010; Littleton and Mercer 2010; Littleton and Mercer 2013).

In Chapter 1, we described how the discussions we have observed among students working in groups can be seen to be related to three types of talk: Disputational, Cumulative, and Exploratory. We provided three examples of group discussions to illustrate this typology. Talk resembling the first two types is quite common, but Exploratory Talk (also known as 'accountable talk': Resnick 1999) is quite rare. Yet it typifies the kind of talk that is associated with successful collaborative learning. To put it simply, students need to learn how to use talk to reason together – to use Exploratory Talk; and they may never accomplish this unless they are helped to do so by their teachers. In the *Thinking Together* research, we found that teachers could teach children how to use Exploratory Talk, and that increasing its use in primary classrooms was associated with significantly improved attainment for the children involved, as measured by tests of reasoning and curriculum-related assessments in mathematics and science.

In one typical study of this series, seven classes of children aged nine to ten in primary schools were first of all inducted into effective ways of working in groups. They were guided by their teachers into constructing and using a set of ground rules for talking and working together, which would generate Exploratory Talk. Qualitative and quantitative assessments of children's group discussions, before and after they had received this guidance, showed that children in these 'target' classes began to use much more Exploratory Talk. This focus on talk for collective thinking was maintained as they were taught mathematics and science for the next eight months, with teachers using a 'dialogic' approach that emphasized classroom discussion, group work and the development of children's awareness of talking for learning. A total of 109 children completed the programme, and a further 121 children in 'control' classes completed the same mathematics curriculum without any change in teaching style.

By examining the talk of children working together, we not only found that the groups in the target classes came to use more Exploratory Talk, but that those using it most tended to achieve the best solutions to problems. An analysis of the kind described in Chapters 1 and 4, using concordance software to measure the relative incidence of key reasoning words in children's talk over time, showed that words such as 'because', 'if' and 'why' became more common in the talk of the target children who had been taught to use the ground rules for generating Exploratory Talk. Children in both sets of classes, target and control, were also given tests on their learning of curriculum subjects before and after the intervention period, based on the Standard Assessment Tasks (SATs) that were then used throughout English state schools to assess children's attainment at ages ten to 11. The pre/post SATs scores for mathematics and science showed a significantly higher improvement for children in target classes than those in the matched control classes.

Our finding that Exploratory Talk helps children's study of school subjects was important, but equally interesting was the finding that the children in target classes also showed significantly greater improvements in non-verbal reasoning over the period of the intervention, as assessed by a widely-accepted metric – the Raven's Progressive Matrices test (Raven, Court & Raven 1995). A study led by some of our colleagues (Wegerif, Perez, Rojas-Drummond, Mercer & Velez 2005) obtained similar results from a project in Mexican schools. While the target class children's Raven's test scores increased over the period of the intervention, the control children's actually decreased. Moreover, further research in Mexico by Rojas-Drummond, Mazón, Littleton and Vélez (2012) found that children who were taught to use Exploratory Talk went on to write better, more logical summaries of texts they had read compared with those produced by students in control classes in which no such teaching was provided.

Explanations of the effects of interthinking on individual reasoning

When we discussed the results of the *Thinking Together* research in our previous book (Mercer & Littleton 2007), we proposed that there were three possible types of explanation for how involvement in Exploratory Talk during group work could promote the development of individual children's reasoning skills. We called these explanations *appropriation, co-construction* and *transformation*. We have since tried to refine these explanations and we will draw on that more recent work (Mercer 2013) here. The three explanations represent a series of relatively stronger theoretical claims about the role of language and joint activity in the development of children's ability to reason. We will consider each in turn.

1. *Appropriation*: During group work, if they use Exploratory Talk, children can learn successful problem solving strategies from each other and go on to apply them, as individuals, in any subsequent relevant situation. This represents a relatively weak claim for the influence of joint activity on individual thinking, because it merely identifies other people as sources of useful knowledge. Language plays an important role here, but only in so much as it is a medium for transmitting knowledge from one mind to another.

2. *Co-construction*: By using Exploratory Talk to coordinate their mental efforts, children may not only share ideas but also argue about them. By interthinking, they can jointly construct new, effective strategies for completing a task that are better than any of them might have devised alone. Individuals can then go on to use these new effective strategies when they subsequently encounter similar problems. This represents a stronger claim for the influence of social (intermental) activity on individual (intramental) learning and development, because it locates the genesis of effective cognitive strategies in collective reasoning, and not just in individual minds. Individuals in a group can also gain new levels of understanding through co-construction, if they jointly construct new explanations with their partners.

3. *Transformation*: Using Exploratory Talk will not only help children to reason together; especially if they self-consciously adopt ground rules for talk agreed with their teacher, it will promote their metacognitive awareness of how they talk and reason together. It is also likely to stimulate their 'theory of mind' capacities, as they become more aware of what other students think and of any contradictions with their own points of view. It can thus encourage them to take what the psychologists Muller-Mirza and Perret-Clermont (2009) call a 'reflective stance' when considering their own and others' ideas. Children can then internalize the reasoned discussion of Exploratory Talk as a model for reasoning alone. They become able to have a kind of reasoned dialogue with themselves ('On the one hand ... but on the other hand ... '). Their

intramental thinking will be transformed, through intermental activity, to become more dialogic. This would represent the achievement of a higher form of reasoning, which enables children to assess problems and issues in a more critical, detached way, and to monitor and regulate their own problem-solving when doing a task on their own.

All three explanations link the use of spoken dialogue to the development of reasoning. Each also links the distinctive human capacities for sharing information, assessing common knowledge and planning goal-directed activity to the ways children learn and develop cognitively and socially. Each represents a possible way that useful knowledge and cognitive skills can be disseminated among members of a community. They are not mutually exclusive, and any one of them could account for the effects of collaborative learning on individual learning and achievement under some circumstances. But while the 'appropriation' explanation is quite prosaic, the 'co-construction'and'transformation'explanations are not.'Co-construction' is interesting because it implies the application of some 'collective intelligence' (Woolley Chabrsi, Pentland, Hashmi & Malone 2010), which can achieve more than individuals can alone. The 'transformation' explanation is the most intriguing, though, because it links the culturally-based, social use of language with psychological development, in accord with Vygotsky's (1962, 1978) claims as we explained in Chapter 1. Our interpretation of the basic process involved is represented in Figure 5.1.

Figure 5.1 represents the relationship between language experience and cognitive development. Being in two dimensions, the figure may seem to show this process as cyclical, but we intend it to be seen as a kind of *helix*, extending through time rather than space. Children are born into a social

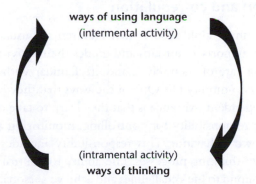

ways of using language
(intermental activity)

(intramental activity)
ways of thinking

FIGURE 5.1 The Vygotskian relationship between social language use and cognitive development

world, in which they become involved in dialogues with other people even before they are fluent speakers of a language. As they engage with people around them, and begin to acquire language, they will hear those people using language to make sense of the world. Children do not only commonly experience life in the company of other people, the people around them will often offer children an account of that shared experience. They do so using the 'ways of using language' in Figure 5.1 that act as models for children's own developing ways of making sense. This is a dialogic process: children can use the ways with words that they learn to put their own accounts of experience into the conversation, and ask questions about what they are experiencing. The ways they come to make sense of the world are thus shaped by the knowledge that they hear encoded in language, and by their own active use of language with others as a joint, sense-making tool. And as children learn and develop into adults, their active contributions to the dialogues of their community can add to its shared knowledge and change its social practices, including the ways that language is used within it. Any useful new ideas and ways with words they create can become, in turn, part of the cultural common knowledge of their community and so available as resources for the sense making and language practices of their own children. The process is thus not just one of cultural acquisition and reproduction, but a creative process, of cultural renewal. (As an aside, we might note that this is why the cultural function of universities cannot be reduced to that of advanced teaching; they have the equally important role of enabling new, advanced, creative thinking by each new generation of scholars to be incorporated into the communities of discourse of each subject area.)

Talk and the development of self-regulation, metacognition and co-regulation

The nature of human childhood is that children are usually born into a community that supports, constrains and guides their activity until they are capable of taking care of themselves, and are familiar with the normative requirements of community life. One of the ways that they become capable of relatively independent existence is that they learn to take over (from their adult carers) the responsibility for controlling, monitoring and reflectively assessing their own behaviour. This responsibility includes being able to control their own thinking processes. The ability to control one's thoughts and actions to respond to life's challenges and achieve personal goals is known as *self-regulation* (Zimmerman 2008; Whitebread & Pino-Pasternak 2010). The line of research that has investigated the development of self-regulation has, like much of psychology, had as its prime focus a more individualistic concern; how becoming able to self-regulate is linked to a child's cognitive development and learning. Winne and Hadwin (2008) define effective self-regulators as those who set goals and make plans for their learning, monitor their progress toward their goals and revise their strategies for reaching their goals as necessary. Self-regulation necessarily involves *metacognition*, thinking about thinking, because it requires reflective consideration of one's own actions. Research suggests that the ability to self-regulate while problem-solving may be a significant determinant of effective learning (Veenman & Spaans 2005; Whitebread & Pino Pasternak *op. cit.*).

Self-regulation is, by definition, concerned with individual behaviour. In the context of interthinking, however, a related concept from developmental psychology becomes relevant, which we introduced in Chapter 1 and used to discuss children's group activity at the interactive whiteboard in Chapter 4. This is *co-regulation* (Volet, Summers & Thurman 2009). The term *shared regulation* has also been used by developmental psychologists to describe the 'constant monitoring and regulation of joint activity, which cannot be reduced to mere individual activity' (Vauras, Iiskala, Kajamies, Kinnunen & Lehtinen 2003: 35), but our preference is for 'co-regulation' because it captures better the joint quality of the thinking involved.

As we explained in Chapter 1, a distinctive feature of human cognition, grounded in our evolutionary history, is that we can combine our individual cognitive capacities into a collective thinking capacity: we are able to use language and other modes of communication to solve problems together. We are born with 'social brains' that enable us not only to interact and manage complex social relationships, but to interthink in ways other animals cannot. As Vygotsky suggested, this means that learning ways of thinking collectively and of thinking alone are, for humans, aspects of the same developmental process. Any theory of human cognition, and of its development, must deal with both its intermental and its intramental nature.

Following Vygotsky, Wertsch (1979, 1985) proposed that children's experiences of being regulated could provide a template for regulating their own behaviour. Thus he described how a child who is guided and instructed through a logical set of procedures for solving a certain kind of problem can internalize those procedures as a way of solving such problems alone. That is, the child creates internal, psychological correlates for the external, social mechanisms that have regulated their behaviour in the earliest years. Figure 5.2 is a basic representation of this intermental–intramental process, which has the same helical form as the process shown in Figure 5.1.

Figure 5.2 depicts children's experience of being regulated as a model for their self-regulation, but as with Figure 5.1, the process has a helical,

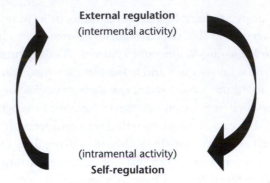

External regulation
(intermental activity)

(intramental activity)
Self-regulation

FIGURE 5.2 The Vygotskian relationship between external, social regulation and the development of self-regulation

progressive form. As they become more self-regulative, and also learn from ways that they have been regulated, children become able to exert some regulative control over other people. Moreover, they become able to engage in the co-regulation of activities with others.

Vygotsky proposed that there were strong connections between the processes represented in Figures 5.1 and 5.2. For example, he suggested that young children's common use of private or 'egocentric' speech for talking themselves through a problem was an echo of external regulation, and that this illustrated the way language functions as both a cultural tool and a psychological tool. Wertsch's research, mentioned above, showed that if children are 'talked through' a strategy for solving a problem by an adult, they then often become able to talk themselves through the same kind of problem; and even when they eventually do not need to talk aloud to think, they may nevertheless still be using language-based procedures for thinking. In a recent appraisal of Vygotsky's work, Miller (2011: 370) puts it as follows: 'not only can I instruct you and be instructed by you, but I can also instruct myself, and this function of inner speech is the basis for self-regulation'.

We can now link up the two figures, 5.1 and 5.2. If a group of children working on a task in a group engage in Exploratory Talk, they are simultaneously reasoning together and co-regulating their activity, using the cultural and cognitive tool of spoken language. They are employing a functional language genre they have appropriated from the cultural resources of their community to interthink. If they invoke the ground rules for Exploratory Talk during their discussion – for example, to highlight that one participant's voice is not being heard, or that reasons to support a particular idea or solution to a problem need to be articulated – they are also demonstrating a reflective awareness of how to co-regulate the process of interthinking they are involved in. Their intermental activity, of reasoning together and co-regulating, provides a model for the intramental activity of reasoning alone and self-regulating one's own problem-solving activities. This is a sociocultural explanation of the development of individual intellectual capacities, and one that is in accord with the findings of available research.

On the basis of our recent research on the use of interactive whiteboards in primary schools described in Chapter 4, we have suggested that children's initial invocation of the ground rules and principles of Exploratory Talk may represent a transition phase, during which the responsibility for co-regulation is transferred to the group (Warwick, Mercer & Kershner 2013). Our suggestion is that the transfer of responsibility for engaging in Exploratory Talk progresses through three phases – teacher responsibility, joint responsibility and student responsibility. A teacher initially helps the children set up their group work, providing external, guiding regulatory assistance that is enshrined in the ground rules for talk. However, the ground rules do not merely provide an initial, temporary support for children's collective interthinking; they provide an enduring system for co-regulating group work in the future. At first children may use the ground rules in a somewhat mechanical, literal way; but over time they come to incorporate them into their collective thinking in ways that are dialogic, dynamic and continuous, with the participants regulating their activity through the responsive and reciprocal ways in which they use language. Our suggestion is that people of any age can go through a similar, transformative process in learning to be more effective interthinkers.

Why does interthinking sometimes get better results than individual thinking?

We have provided a sociocultural account of how interthinking helps children's cognitive development and learning. We now will try to use the same sociocultural framework to explain how and why, in everyday life, thinking together can be better for achieving creative solutions to problems than individual efforts. In the earlier part of this chapter we proposed that there were three possible explanations for why children's involvement in Exploratory Talk helps to develop their reasoning skills: *appropriation*, *co-construction* and *transformation*. Similar kinds of explanations can be offered for understanding why and when collective thinking can be productive in the work settings and other situations discussed in Chapters 2, 3 and 4. In this case, we are not concerned with the effects of collective cognition on individual learning or development, but rather with why groups can – under the right conditions – achieve better and more creative solutions to problems than individuals, so we need to adapt the explanations accordingly. We will consider each in turn.

1. *Appropriation*: By using a mode of interaction resembling Cumulative Talk, members of a group can share relevant information and problem-solving strategies. Some members may know a good strategy for tackling a particular kind of problem, while others may not. Other relevant knowledge may also be distributed among members of the group, with no one member having all of it. They can share that information by talking to each other. By pooling all their knowledge and expertise, the group may be more able to solve a problem than any of its individual members would on their own. No dialogic interthinking process is necessarily involved, because all that is involved is the use of talk (and possibly other modes of representation) for transmitting information with some acceptable degree of accuracy from one mind to another.

2. *Co-construction*: By using the kind of dialogue represented by Exploratory Talk to co-regulate their mental efforts, members of a group can share and combine ideas. Such collaborative discussion, in which ideas are challenged and reasons offered in the pursuit of a common goal, is likely to lead them to select the best strategies for solving the problems from the options offered by members of the group, and apply them to the task in hand. They can also argue productively to construct new, robust, generalizable strategies together for completing the task that were better than any of them would have achieved alone. Their successful achievements would reflect what has been called the 'assembly bonus effect', whereby the performance of a group is better than that of its best member (Laughlin, Hatch, Silver & Boh 2004). This explains the benefits of teamwork through the dynamics of collaborative activity, and not just through the pooling of the resources that exist in individual heads. In these circumstances, language is not only a medium for sharing knowledge, but for constructing it and regulating the constructive interthinking process.

3. *Transformation*: If dialogue resembling Exploratory Talk takes place within a group, the interactions among members will enable them to share relevant information, co-regulate their activities and co-construct good solutions to problems. But that the experience can also develop the skills of members in reasoning collectively, so that they become more skilled at interthinking. Engaging in Exploratory Talk can stimulate the group members' theory of mind capabilities, so that they become more aware of the possibility of different points of view. They can jointly reflect on the adequacy of the ground rules they are using to talk and work together, and they can monitor and improve their efforts

accordingly. This enables a group's activities to be co-regulated with increasing effectiveness. Over time, the metacognitive nature of their interactions enables them to become a more creative, productive group than they had been before. This then feeds into the kinds of progressive, developmental helix we represented by Figures 5.1 and 5.2. In this situation, language is not only used by the group to share information, and to co-construct good solutions to problems, but also as a tool for joint, reflective, critical consideration of how members work together.

When applied to cognitive development, these are not mutually exclusive explanations of the potentially positive outcomes of using Exploratory Talk. They could all apply in a given situation, to a lesser or greater extent, depending on the nature of a task and the dynamics of the group tackling it. However, they have rather different implications for how groups can be helped to work most effectively. *Appropriation* implies only that group members should try to be as clear and precise in their transmission of information to other members of the group, so interaction resembling Cumulative Talk might serve well enough. *Co-construction* implies that group members need to use Exploratory Talk, so that they generate an explicit reasoned discussion to help them to assess ideas and proposals critically and equitably, so that the best solutions (rather than those of the most vocal or articulate members) are pursued. *Transformation* also requires the use of Exploratory Talk, but in addition members of a group must engage in some metacognition, reflecting on their collective thinking processes and use of talk, and use those reflections to try and improve their group dynamics.

Two of these explanations imply that Exploratory Talk is the most effective form of dialogue for interthinking, and in general we would say that this is the case. Reviewing research on working groups in Chapter 2, research on computer-mediated communication in Chapter 4 and on the creative discussions of performance arts in Chapter 3 all lead us to this general conclusion. However, the 'appropriation' explanation would support the view that Exploratory talk is not always needed. For example, our recent work analyzing children's creative story writing indicates that for open-ended, divergent tasks where there is no 'right' answer, a form of Cumulative Talk in which children integrate, elaborate and/or reformulate each other's contributions to negotiate meaning without necessarily engaging in explicit, reasoned argument has been found to generate successful outcomes (Rojas-Drummond, Albarrán & Littleton 2008; Rojas-Drummond, Littleton, Hernandez & Zúñiga 2010). Different types of collaborative task implicate different kinds of talk, with convergent tasks (focused on finding one right answer) tending to generate more Exploratory

Talk than divergent tasks (which have more open-ended outcomes) even among groups that are working well together. Cumulative Talk can be very effective for achieving certain useful and creative outcomes, as we noted regarding the creative artists in Chapter 3 and as we have seen with primary school children who use it during 'thought showers' intended to generate an initial, possible set of ideas for writing creatively together (Vass, Littleton, Miell & Jones 2008). Different genres of talk will have different functionalities – though it is difficult to think why anyone should want to actively encourage more Disputational Talk, at least in terms of achieving better creative outcomes from group-based activity.

Research has not yet provided us with evidence that would enable us to say, with any certainty, which of the three explanations is most relevant for understanding the processes of collective thinking that take place in any specific context. However, we have identified some of the obstacles to effective and creative problem-solving by teams or problems that commonly arise when people work together. These include failing to include all members and listen to all points of view, deferring to the views of high status group members without other rational support for those views, individual members withholding relevant information, and a group reaching superficial agreement without serious consideration of the relevant range of options. In Chapter 2 we discussed the phenomenon of 'groupthink', whereby such problems can lead to poor decision making, even by highly qualified people working on issues of supreme importance.

On the basis of our review of relevant research, we can also draw some conclusions of interest to anyone wishing to ensure the most productive and creative outcomes from group-based activity. In summary, group members should:

- know how to generate and sustain Exploratory Talk;
- recognize the value of that kind of interaction for achieving good outcomes from their collective work;
- recognize the value of regularly reflecting upon and reviewing the ways they are working together, against the standard of relevant criteria, which would represent the agreed ground rules for how group members should interact.

Such ground rules would include:

- all voices in the group are heard and taken into account;
- all relevant ideas and information are shared and justified with reasons whenever possible;

- ideas and proposals offered can (and should) be criticized if there are good reasons to do so;
- members know that ideas can be expressed openly in a atmosphere of mutual trust, in the interests of achieving the group's collective success;
- the group should use equitable discussion to try to seek consensus about any outcomes for which they are jointly responsible.

Even groups who have been working successfully together for a while, or new groups whose members have already developed the necessary social and linguistic skills for thinking collectively, would be advised to continue to reflect metacognitively on the communication within their group, to help ensure that they are using their collective intellectual resources to best effect.

Creative interthinking: a sociocultural perspective

We will now draw on the three explanations offered earlier for how and why collective thinking can be productive, and apply in understanding collaborative creativity. Perhaps one of the reasons why language-based processes of creative interthinking are not well understood is that the initial and most influential psychological studies of creativity and creative processes have, like those of problem-solving and learning, been focused on the abilities and achievements of individuals. Researchers have typically tried to assess an individual's creativity/creative potential, or to characterize the nature of the individual creative processes. This reflects the dominant conception of creative thinking as an intramental process, rather than intermental. In Western culture, at least, the capacity for 'being creative' is typically ascribed to individual talent and seen as involving an individual producing 'a new mental combination that is expressed in the world' Sawyer (2012: 7). If we are to understand the complexity and the diversity of creativity, and especially if we want to maximize opportunities for it to be achieved, then we need to widen the focus from the individual as lone creator to recognize that creative achievement normally involves the collective intellectual efforts of a group of people. Creative thinking can of course be pursued *intra*mentally, but it commonly only reaches fruition through *inter*mental activity as people 'interthink' in pursuit of some common interests. We have discussed many examples of this, taken from our own research and that of others, in Chapter 3.

Not all research on creativity has been focused on individuals. There is a growing body of work that adopts a sociocultural approach to creativity. Researchers taking this perspective share a recognition of the intrinsically social and communicative nature of human life, and usually argue for the existence of a special, reciprocal relationship between intermental and intramental activity. Thus communication, thinking, creativity, learning and development are all treated as processes shaped by cultural and historical factors, whereby knowledge is shared and new understandings, ideas, artefacts and meanings are jointly constructed.

Some of the earliest sociocultural work challenged individualistic conceptions of creativity by pointing to the significance of the social and cultural context within which people celebrated for their creativity have worked (see, for example, Moran 2010). Creativity can be construed as a collaborative accomplishment (mediated by cultural tools, technologies and artefacts), one that is generated by the interactions and relationships in which creative activity takes place. Vera John-Steiner (2000, 2006) has explored the nature and significance of collaborative creative relationships within different fields, including sciences and the arts. She suggests that 'generative ideas emerge from joint thinking, from significant conversations, and from sustained shared struggles to achieve new insights by partners in thought' (John-Steiner 2000: 3) and has used the reflective accounts of creative partners to describe how the interplay between them contributes to the creative process and its outputs. Working with diverse data sources, including the analysis of focused interviews, biographical data and the reconstruction of partnerships through joint narrative accounts, she identified four patterns of creative collaborative partnership, which she terms distributed collaboration, complementary collaboration, family collaboration and integrative collaboration.

The first collaborative pattern – *distributed collaboration* – involves the informal, voluntary exchange of information and ideas between people who share similar interests often in casual settings, such as in conversations at conferences. Such conversations are spontaneous and responsive and 'may lead to new personal insights. When exchanges become heated or controversial, new groups may form to address issues in greater depth. Other groups splinter or dissolve. But out of such informal connections some lasting partnerships may be built' (John-Steiner 2000: 198). The second pattern – *complementary collaboration* – is, John-Steiner suggests, the most widely practiced form of collaboration and is characterized by a clear division of labour, overlapping values and complementarity, be this of expertise, disciplinary knowledge or roles. The third pattern – *family collaboration* – is a mode of interaction in which roles are fluid and flexible and liable to change over time. Participants are committed to each other for a sustained period of time and they trust each other and share a common vision. They help each other to shift roles, for instance in moving from the position of novice to a more expert level.

One of John-Steiner's central claims is that truly transformative thinking or the co-construction of, for example, a new art form, thrives best in long-term *integrative collaborations*, the fourth pattern identified. Collaborators in such partnerships share a visionary commitment and a desire to transform existing practices, knowledge and approaches into new visions and ways of working.

This non-hierarchical characterization of creative work is intended to allow for the possibility of movement and change among patterns. Although each pattern is valued and valuable, John-Steiner suggests that truly transformative changes happen through integrative collaboration. While she did not undertake any detailed analyses of collaborators' dialogue, John-Steiner recognized that it is a complex interactional accomplishment that 'requires the shaping of a shared language, the pleasures and risks of honest dialogue and the search for common ground' (John-Steiner 2000: 204).

We can make some connections here between John-Steiner's four types of collaboration and our three earlier explanations of successful interthinking – appropriation, co-construction and transformation. The success of the distributed type of collaboration might be explained, at least in part, by appropriation. Those involved will share information and act in complementary ways to achieve a task, but their commitments to the joint activity, especially in distributed collaboration, may be temporary and expedient. Distributed partners might be *cooperating*, but not truly *collaborating*. Success through a complementary type of collaboration might also be explained by appropriation, though the more long-term commitment to the joint endeavour and shared values might be thought more likely to generate co-construction.

The success of her third and fourth types, family collaboration and integrative collaboration, would seem to be linked with co-construction and with transformation, as we have described them. Indeed, John-Steiner says that integrated collaborations transform the individual involved. Those relationships have a continuing, metacognitive, reflective quality whereby partners see the progressive development of their working relationship as part of their joint endeavour. Such relationships might regularly involve the use of talk of an exploratory kind – though the fact that integrative relationships are built upon a firm foundation of common knowledge might mean that the partners do not have to be as explicit in its references and reasons as in the archetypal form of Exploratory Talk, because they can safely take so much relevant knowledge for granted.

Through combining these ideas, we move a little further towards understanding the ways dialogue can help people think creatively together, as they work and talk collaboratively over time. But what is it that they achieve through talk, at certain points in their activity, which enables creativity? With this question in mind, we offer a new concept – that of the intermental creativity zone.

The Intermental Creativity Zone

In our research on teaching and learning in school, we wanted to conceptualize the way that a teacher and a student, or group of students, could create and maintain a shared focus, over time, on a learning objective – say, using a mathematical procedure, understanding the plot of a novel, or describing and explaining the results of an experiment. We were already aware of Vygotsky's concept of the Zone of Proximal Development (ZPD), which – to oversimplify a little – represents an area of extended understanding into which a teacher can draw the thinking of a student through sensitive, 'scaffolded' instruction. Although useful, the ZPD does not really capture the temporal, dynamic, dialogic nature of the process involved, whereby it is essential that teacher and learner(s) strive to build and extend a foundation of common knowledge to support their activities. When classroom talk achieves this, teaching-and-learning is like a track-laying vehicle that carries with it the resources for its own progress – though it is unlike any conventional vehicle in that the tracks are constantly being renewed and refined to suit the intended journey.

We suggest that something similar must happen in other situations, when people of any age are working together to create new ideas and understandings. They use talk and joint activity to create a shared resource of ideas that can be jointly considered, and a framework for collected working that will enable their work to progress. Our colleague Rupert Wegerif (2007) calls this virtual resource of ideas a 'dialogic space'. In the context of the classroom, the framework is provided by the ground rules that govern interactions between teachers and students, and among students, which are related to their roles in pursuing educational goals. Other types of social situation will involve the use of different sets of ground rules.

In earlier publications (Mercer 2000; Mercer & Littleton 2007; Mercer 2008), we have used the concept of the *Intermental Development Zone* (IDZ) for helping conceptualize how a teacher and a learner can stay attuned to each other's changing states of knowledge and understanding over the course of an educational activity. For teaching and learning to happen, teacher and learner must use talk and joint activity to create and negotiate a particular kind of dialogic space, the IDZ, which is built from the contextual foundation of their common knowledge and aims. In the 'bubble' of this Intermental Development Zone, which is reconstituted constantly as the dialogue of their activity continues, teacher and learner negotiate their pursuit of education. If the quality of the Zone is successfully maintained, the teacher can enable a learner to reach new levels of knowledge, understanding and skill. If the dialogue fails to keep the minds mutually attuned, the IDZ collapses and the learning grinds to a halt. The IDZ represents a continuing state of shared consciousness, focused on the task in hand and dedicated to the objective of learning.

The enabling of learning by some members of the group by other more expert members is not the main issue in some kinds of collaborative learning and problem-solving, especially in workplace settings, so we cannot use the IDZ concept to explain collective creativity there. Instead, for groups of people of more equal status we could imagine the existence of a similar phenomenon, an *intermental creativity zone* (ICZ) that is established on the dynamic, developing basis of relevant common knowledge and affords a contextual foundation for their work together. In this ICZ, reconstituted constantly as the dialogue unfolds, collaborators negotiate their way through the joint activity in which they are involved using appropriate linguistic tools – such as specialized discourses. The ICZ is thus a continuing event of contextualized, co-regulated joint activity – the product of a process of interthinking that involves a reflective and metacognitive orientation to collective work that is likely to involve some agreed common goals, rules and ways of working (which may be challenged/revised over time). It is supported by a foundation of common knowledge, but a foundation that is continually being rebuilt. Its quality is dependent, to a large degree, to the abilities of those involved to use their 'theory of mind' capacities to appraise what other people know and do not know, what their intentions are and how they are contributing to the group's activity. Like the IDZ, the ICZ helps to conceptualize the ways that collaborators use language to travel together from the past (from what was or is) into the future (to what might be).

Interthinking concepts

In this final chapter, we thought it might be helpful to summarize the main concepts we have used in our account of the process of thinking collectively:

1. *Interthinking*: This means using talk to pursue collective intellectual activity. It represents an important and distinctive strength of human cognition, whereby people can combine their intellectual resources to achieve more through working together than any individual could do on their own. This emergent affordance of the human brain, at least

as much as its capacities for processing information, inferring the intentions of others and understanding complex social arrangements, is likely to have played a crucial role in the evolutionary survival of our ancestors.

2. *Language*: Available evidence from neuroscience and psychological studies encourages the view that language is not a specific, modular capacity of the human brain but is fully integrated with cognition as a whole. Although other modes of communication and representation can have an important role in interthinking, language has a special role because it enables people to engage in reasoned dialogue. Other modes of communication cannot enable that, in any comparable sense. Moreover, experience of involvement in ways of using language for thinking collectively provide models for children on how to think alone.

3. *Intermental and intramental activity*: Sociocultural theory proposes that there is a vital link between the development of children's language skills, their involvement in the social interaction of everyday life (intermental activity) and the development of their individual cognition (intramental activity). The results of our own and other research, as described earlier in this chapter, not only support the existence of that link but suggest that it is even stronger than had previously been thought, with language playing a vital role in the development and maintenance of that link. Our own research highlights the connection between children being inducted into language genres that resemble Exploratory Talk and the development of their ability to reason. In brief, thinking collectively provides a template for thinking alone. This statement has important educational implications, but those implications have not been given the kind of recognition in educational policy and practice that they deserve.

4. *Common knowledge*: Successful interthinking requires partners to have, and to develop, a foundation of common knowledge to underpin their discussions. We have distinguished two types of common knowledge, both of which can be important. The first of these is accumulated through the activities of a group, as members develop a shared history. They have knowledge in common because it has been generated by their joint activities and associated conversations. It is the kind of common knowledge that allows a speaker to refer only briefly to the content of a previous conversation and expect listeners to have some recollection of what it had been about. We have called this *dynamic common knowledge*, because it is produced by the dynamics of the group's own extended activity. The second type, which we call *background common knowledge*, is

that which any established member of a community of practice can take for granted as being shared with other members and does not therefore need to be explained from first principles. It is the kind of knowledge that enables any two physicists, Beatles fans or people who have grown up in the same town to take certain kinds of understanding for granted, even if they have never met before.

5.   *Ground rules*: The creative process of problem-solving is best pursued through a form of language based on normative ground rules, which, by ensuring that group discussion is effectively co-regulated, allow and encourage the sharing of new ideas and their critical examination, while avoiding the risk of personal attacks on those who offer new ideas or criticize them. All types of social interaction involve such ground rules, but the relevant issues here are whether or not they are part of the common knowledge of a group and fit for purpose. Group activity often goes awry because members are not all following the same ground rules, or because they are following inappropriate ones. For ground rules to be effective, they need not only to be appropriate but to be collectively generated and owned by the group. Group members need to recognize the rules as the regulative basis for their activity – though the rules can be reviewed and revised if that is agreed as useful.

6.   *Exploratory Talk*: As we have defined it, Exploratory Talk represents a social mode of reasoning. It is sometimes called 'accountable talk' or 'collaborative reasoning'. It is a cultural linguistic tool, a genre for helping a group of people achieve creative, justifiable solutions to some common kinds of problems. It will not suit all kinds of collective endeavour, or all phases of a collaborative activity, but it is a good example of how talk can be shaped to suit its purpose by group members working to an appropriate set of ground rules. It is underpinned by partners taking a metacognitive, reflective stance on their activities, being self-aware of how they work together and being able to co-regulate their activities successfully. We contrasted Exploratory Talk with Cumulative Talk and Disputational Talk, arguing that while Cumulative Talk can also be useful in some situations, discussion resembling Exploratory Talk is usually necessary if collective thinking is to be productive and problems such as 'groupthink' (as discussed in Chapter 2) are to be avoided. Despite its functional value, however, observations of groups working together suggest Exploratory Talk is not as commonly used as one might expect.

7.   *Appropriation*: To be successful, collective, creative problem-solving will involve a group of people sharing relevant information among themselves, so that what was originally private, individual knowledge becomes common knowledge. We have called the process by which

individual members learn from each other *appropriation*, and its success will depend on how good group members are at explaining what they know and interpreting and remembering what they hear. This is the kind of language use that has figured most in influential explanations of the relationship between language, cognition and collective activity; but in our view it is not the most interesting or important.

8. *Co-construction*: Although the sharing of relevant knowledge is almost bound to be an important feature, the success of group activity is likely to also involve a more complex kind of interaction. This is the process we have called *co-construction*, whereby members of a group use a process of reasoned argument to examine, in a critical way, any ideas offered and compare possible options for how they should proceed to a successful conclusion. It depends on participants using their 'theory of mind' capacities to good effect to appreciate the relative extent of common knowledge within a group, and to use ways of interacting that are appropriate for pursuing their joint aims at any particular time (such as Cumulative Talk or Exploratory Talk). This co-construction process can generate new ideas, new problem-solving strategies and solutions that none of the individual members possessed before they began to interact.

9. *Transformation*: A third process may also be involved, which depends on the distinctive human ability for metacognition – thinking about thinking. The reflective, metacognitive insights of the members of a co-constructive group about how they have gone about tackling a problem and managing their discussions about it can be used as a resource for future planning. This can enable a group of people to treat their joint task as not only being the achievement of a solution to a given problem, but also how to co-regulate their activities effectively. It may result in what we have called *transformation*, whereby the group becomes a more effective and creative problem-solving team than it was originally.

10. *The Intermental Creativity Zone*: We have introduced this term to represent the way that partners engaged in co-constructing new knowledge generate a continuing, dynamic, referential framework for their talk about their joint endeavour. As a group of people begin to work together, the ICZ will be constructed from the resources of their existing common knowledge, which may need to be established through initial stages of dialogue. However, as the dialogue progresses, that common knowledge is being constantly accumulated and revised through their talk and other joint meaning-making activity. This can be a problematic process, and the 'bubble' of the ICZ that encapsulates their interthinking

may collapse if it is not properly maintained through their joint efforts. If it is maintained, it can enable the cognitive capacities of the individual members of the group to be combined into a collective cognitive capability that is superior to that of any individual members.

Conclusions

In this book we have described, and tried to explain, the phenomenon of interthinking – the everyday process whereby people collectively and creatively use talk to solve problems and make joint sense of the world. We have described what research has revealed about what makes it successful, and what makes it fail. To do so, we have often had to extrapolate from the findings of research that was not explicitly about interthinking because, surprisingly, there have not really been any other concerted attempts to explain it. However, as in Chapters 2 and 3 we have been able to draw on a range of studies from various lines of enquiry.

In Chapter 1 we described recent work in evolutionary psychology through which the concept of the 'social brain' has been developed to represent the social capabilities of human cognition. The focus of that work has mainly been on the emergent capability of our ancestors to organize and make sense of a complex society, and to defend their interests by being able to second-guess or argue against the intentions of other, potentially competitive, individuals. We argued that an evolutionary account of the success of our species should also consider the possibility of our ancestors becoming better at surviving through the evolution of a capacity to think productively and creatively together in small groups. This is something that members of other species, even our primate relatives, patently cannot do. Once a group of hominids could use language to review and plan their techniques for survival, they would have an advantage over any competitors. Incorporating the language-based capacity for interthinking into an account of human evolution is clearly more compatible with existing accounts that emphasize the importance of collaboration and communal survival than those that emphasize individual competition and survival.

In Chapter 4 we described how computer-based digital technologies can, when used in conjunction with language, provide useful opportunities and support for people to think collectively, whether in the same location or through online talk at a distance. Digital technology is particularly useful because of the ways it can enable people to communicate and record the development and products of a discussion in mutually accessible forms, at a distance or after a discussion has ended. However, better technology will not, in itself, improve the quality of interthinking. The same kinds of constraints and potential problems apply to people using technology to work together in face-to-face groups, and to virtual groups working at a distance, as apply in more traditional situations, and the same approach can be used to help overcome them.

In several parts of the book we have referred to research on creativity. We are certainly not alone in suggesting that the creative power of collective thinking cannot be explained only by reference to individual contributions or talents of those involved. It is now well accepted that the story of the lone genius, struggling to have a brilliant new idea accepted against the conventional resistance of all of those around, has limited explanatory value. There is clear evidence that the most successfully creative individuals have usually benefited from being members of communities of discourse and enquiry, and that groups of people can, and commonly do, make useful creative achievements that none of them would necessarily have achieved alone. However, our argument is that the creative success of group endeavours will depend on the quality of the interthinking that takes place. We have suggested that ensuring the quality of this process will be helped by understanding its nature, and we have identified some of its principal characteristics.

Our own main involvement in the study of interthinking has been motivated by educational concerns. Through that involvement, we have become convinced that the ability to think collectively is one of the most important life skills that education could help children to develop; we have shown that being able to do it effectively is central to activities in many fields of human endeavour. Moreover, as we have explained, there is good evidence in support of the view that learning to use talk to interthink effectively helps to develop children's capacities to think and learn individually.

In this chapter, we have offered a sociocultural perspective on the process of interthinking. The appeal of sociocultural theory, as it has grown from its Vygotskian roots, lies chiefly in its ability to link an explanation of how children are inducted into the cultures of their communities with an explanation of how their individual thinking and understanding develops. Valuable as that is, there is more that it could offer. It might explain how the same intermental processes that enable individual induction into a culture, involving language and other modes of communication, also enable the creative process of cultural renewal and development. It could also transcend the fixation with individual cognition, which still grips most psychology today, and explain the ways that people think collectively. Such a theory would not only help us understand how intermental activity shapes intramental development, but also help us understand collective thinking as an important process in its own right. We hope that we have contributed to the development of such a sociocultural psychology through this book.

We have drawn on a wide range of research studies to explain on the one hand why collective thinking sometimes goes wrong, and on the other how a group of people can use it to achieve better, more creative solutions than any of them would have done alone. On the basis of our own and others' school-based research, we and our colleagues regularly inform teachers about practical ways to help children become better at using talk as a tool for thinking. However, not all children are yet being helped to learn how to interthink. The development of children's spoken language as a tool for thinking collectively is rarely considered an educational priority, compared with the development of their skills in literacy and numeracy. If we want to realise the full potential of our uniquely human ability to think creatively together, this must change.

REFERENCES

Bakhtin, M. (1981) *The Dialogic Imagination*, Austin: University of Texas Press.

Barnes, D. (1976/1992) *From Communication to Curriculum*, Harmondsworth: Penguin (Second edition, 1992, Portsmouth, NH: Boynton/Cook-Heinemann).

Baron, R.S. (2005) 'So right it's wrong: groupthink and the ubiquitous nature of polarized group decision making', *Advances in Experimental Social Psychology*, 37: 219–253.

Bernstein, B. (1971) *Class, Codes and Action Vol. I: theoretical studies towards a sociology of language*, London: Routledge and Kegan Paul.

Bernstein, B. (1975) *Class, Codes and Action Vol. III: towards a theory of educational transmissions*, London: Routledge and Kegan Paul.

Chartrand, T. and Bargh, J. (1999) 'The chameleon effect: the perception–behavior link and social interaction', *Journal of Personality and Social Psychology*, 76 (6): 893–910.

Creese, A. (2008) 'Linguistic ethnography', in K.A. King and N.H. Hornberger (eds), *Encyclopedia of Language and Education, 2nd edn, Volume 10: research methods in language and education*, New York: Springer.

Daniels, H. (2001) *Vygotsky and Pedagogy*, London: Routledge/Falmer.

Daniels, H. (2008) *Vygotsky and Research*, Abingdon: Routledge.

Dawes, L. (2008) *The Essential Speaking and Listening: talk for learning at Key Stage 2*, London: David Fulton.

Dawes, L. (2010) *Creating a Speaking and Listening Classroom: integrating talk for learning at Key Stage 2*, London: David Fulton.

Dawes, L. (2011) *Talking Points: discussion activities in the primary classroom*, London: David Fulton.

Dawes, L. (2013) *Talking Points for Shakespeare Plays: discussion activities for Hamlet, A Midsummer Night's Dream, Romeo and Juliet and Richard III*, London: Taylor and Francis.

Dawes, L., Fisher, E. and Mercer, N. (1992) 'The quality of talk at the computer', *Language and Learning*, October: 22–25.

Dawkins, R. (1976) *The Selfish Gene*, Oxford: Oxford University Press.

Dawkins, R. (2012) 'The descent of Edward Wilson', *Prospect*, May Issue.

Dillenbourg, P. (ed.) (1999) *Collaborative Learning: cognitive and computational approaches*, Oxford: Elsevier Science Ltd.

Dillon, T. (2004) '"It's in the mix, baby": exploring how meaning is created within music technology collaborations', in D. Miell and K. Littleton (eds), *Collaborative Creativity: contemporary perspectives*, London: Free Association Books.

Dirkx, J. and Smith, R. (2004) 'Thinking out of a bowl of spaghetti: learning to learn in online collaborative groups', in T. Roberts (ed), *Online Collaborative Learning: theory and practice*, Hershey, PA: Idea Group.

Dobson, E. (2012) *An Investigation of the Processes of Interdisciplinary Creative Collaboration: the case of music technology students working within the performing arts*, Unpublished PhD thesis: The Open University. [Downloadable from: http://eprints.hud.ac.uk/14689/]. Accessed January 22 2013.

Dobson, E., Flewitt, R., Littleton, K. and Miell, D. (2011) 'Studio-based composers in collaboration: a socioculturally framed study', *Proceedings of the International Computer Music Conference*: 373–376.

Drew, P. and Heritage, J. (eds) (1992) *Talk at Work: interaction in institutional settings*, Cambridge: Cambridge University Press.

Dudley, P. (2013) 'Teacher learning in lesson study', *Teaching and Teacher Education*, 34: 107–121.

Dunbar, R. (1998) 'The social brain hypothesis', *Evolutionary Anthropology*, 6: 178–189.

Edwards, A. (2012) 'The role of common knowledge in achieving collaboration across practices', *Learning, Culture and Social Interaction*, 1 (1): 22–32.

Edwards, D. (1997) *Discourse and Cognition*, London: Sage.

Edwards, D. and Mercer, N. (1987) *Common Knowledge: the development of understanding in the classroom*, London: Methuen/Routledge (Reissued 2012 in the Routledge Revivals series).

Edwards, D. and Middleton, D. (1986) 'Joint remembering: constructing an account of shared experience through conversational discourse', *Discourse Processes*, 9 (4): 423–459.

Edwards, D and Potter, J. (1992) *Discursive Psychology*, London: Sage.

Elbers, E. (1994) 'Sociogenesis and children's pretend play: a variation on Vygotskian themes', in W. de Graaf and R. Maier (eds), *Sociogenesis Re-examined*, New York: Springer.

Esser, J.K. (1998) 'Alive and well after 25 years: a review of groupthink research', *Organizational Behavior and Human Decision Processes*, 73 (2–3): 116–141.

Eteläpelto, A. and Lahti, J. (2008) 'The resources and obstacles of creative collaboration in a long-term learning community', *Thinking Skills and Creativity*, 3(3): 226–240.

Everett, D. (2012) *Language: the cultural tool*, London: Profile Books.

Ferguson, R. (2009) *The Construction of Shared Knowledge through Asynchronous Dialogue*, Unpublished PhD thesis, The Open University. [Downloadable from: http://oro.open.ac.uk/19908]. Accessed January 22 2013.

Ferguson, R., Whitelock, D. and Littleton, K. (2010) 'Improvable objects and attached dialogue: new literacy practices employed by learners to build knowledge together in asynchronous settings', *Digital Culture and Education*, 2 (1): 103–123.

Fiedler, K. and Bless, H. (2001) 'Social cognition', in M. Hewstone and W. Stroebe (eds), *Introduction to Social Psychology*, London: Sage.

Finnegan, R. (2007) *The Hidden Musicians: music-making in an English town (2nd edn)*, Middletown, CT, USA: Wesleyan University Press.

Fivush, R. and Hammond, N.R. (1990) 'Autobiographical memory across the preschool years: toward reconceptualising childhood amnesia', in R. Fivush and J. Hudson (eds), *Knowing and Remembering in Young Children*, New York: Cambridge University Press.

Frith, C. and Singer, T. (2008) 'The role of social cognition in decision making', *Philosophical Transactions of the Royal Society*, 363 (1511): 3875–3886.

Gee, J.P. (2004) *Situated Language and Learning: a critique of traditional schooling*, New York: Routledge.

Gee, J.P. and Green, J. (1998) 'Discourse analysis, learning and social practice: a methodological study', *Review of Research in Education*, 23: 119–169.

Goswami, U. and Bryant, P. (2007) 'Children's cognitive development and learning', *Research Report 2/1a The Primary Review*, Cambridge: University of Cambridge.

Grist, M. (2009) *Changing the Subject: how new ways of thinking about human behavior might change politics, policy and practice*, London: Royal Society of Arts. [Downloadable from: http://www.thersa.org/__data/assets/pdf_file/0020/250625/Nov28th2009 ChangingThe-SubjectPamphlet.pdf]. Accessed 20 December 2012.

Harcourt, A.H. (1988) 'Alliances in contests and social intelligence', in R. Byrne and A. Whiten (eds), *Machiavellian intelligence*, Oxford: Oxford University Press.

Hart, B. and Risley, T. (1995) *Meaningful Differences in the Everyday Experience of Young American Children*, Baltimore, MD: Paul H Brookes Publishing.

Hart, P. (1994) *Government: a study of small groups and policy failure*, Baltimore, MD: The Johns Hopkins University Press.

Heath, S.B. (1982) *Ways with Words: language, life, and work in communities and classrooms*, New York and Cambridge: Cambridge University Press.

Hickey, D.T. (2003) 'Engaged participation versus marginal nonparticipation: a stridently sociocultural approach to achievement motivation', *The Elementary School Journal*, 103 (4): 402–429.

Higgins, S., Mercier, E., Burd, E. and Hatch, A. (2011) 'Multi-touch tables and the relationship with collaborative classroom pedagogies: a synthetic review', *International Journal of Computer-Supported Collaborative Learning*, 6 (4): 515–538.

Hirt, E. and Markman, K. (1995) 'Multiple explanation: a consider-an-alternative strategy for debiasing judgements', *Journal of Personality and Social Psychology*, 69: 1069–1086.

Howe, C. (2010) *Peer Groups and Children's Development*, Oxford: Wiley-Blackwell.

Ingram, A. and Hathorn, L. (2004) 'Methods for Analyzing Collaboration in Online Communications', in T. Roberts (ed), *Online Collaborative Learning: theory and practice*, London: Information Science Publishing.

Janis, I. (1972) *Victims of Groupthink*, New York Houghton Mifflin.

Janis, I. (1982) *Groupthink: psychological studies of policy decisions and fiascoes (2nd edn)*, New York: Houghton Mifflin.

Jeong, H. and Chi, M. (2007) 'Knowledge convergence and collaborative learning', *Instructional Science*, 35: 287–315.

Joffe, S.J. (2007) *The Kinship Coterie and the Literary Endeavours of the Women in the Shelley Circle*, New York: Peter Lang.

John-Steiner, V. (2000) *Creative Collaboration*, New York: Oxford University Press.

John-Steiner, V. (2006) *Creative Collaboration (2nd edn)*, New York: Oxford University Press.

Kress, G. (2010) *Multimodality: a social semiotic approach to contemporary communication*, London: Routledge.

Kress, G. and van Leeuwen T. (1996) *Reading Images: the grammar of visual design*, London: Routledge.

Laughlin, P., Hatch, E., Silver, J. and Boh, L. (2004) 'Groups perform better than the best individuals on letters-to-numbers problems: effects of group size', *Journal of Personality and Social Psychology*, 90 (4): 644–651.

Littleton, K. and Kerawalla, L. (2012) 'Trajectories of inquiry learning', in K. Littleton, E. Scanlon and M. Sharples (eds), *Orchestrating Inquiry Learning*, Abingdon: Routledge.

Littleton, K. and Howe, C. (eds) (2010) *Educational Dialogues: understanding and promoting productive interaction*, London: Routledge.

Littleton, K. and Mercer, N. (2010) 'The significance of educational dialogues between primary school children', in K. Littleton and C. Howe (eds), *Educational Dialogues: understanding and promoting productive interaction*, London: Routledge.

Littleton, K. and Mercer, N. (2012) 'Communication, collaboration and creativity: how musicians negotiate a collective sound', in D. Hargreaves, D. Miell and R. MacDonald (eds), *Musical Imaginations: multidisciplinary perspectives on creativity, performance and perception*, Oxford: Oxford University Press.

Littleton, K. and Mercer, N. (2013) 'Educational dialogues', in K. Hall, T. Cremin, B. Comber and L. Moll (eds), *The Wiley Blackwell International Handbook of Research on Children's Literacy, Learning and Culture*, Oxford: Wiley Blackwell.

Littleton, K., Twiner, A. and Gillen, J. (2010) 'Instruction as orchestration: multimodal connection building with the interactive whiteboard', *Pedagogies: an international journal*, 5 (2): 130–141.

Littleton, K. and Whitelock, D. (2005) 'The negotiation and co-construction of meaning and understanding within a postgraduate online learning community', *Learning, Media and Technology*, 30(2): 147–164.

Martin, J. (1993) 'Genre and literacy: modeling context in educational linguistics', *Annual Review of Applied Linguistics*, 13: 141–172.

Mason, R. (1995) 'Computer conferencing on A423: philosophical problems of equality', *Open University, Centre for Information Technology in Education (CITE)*, Internal Report: 210.

McCaslin, M. (2004) 'Coregulation of opportunity, activity, and identity in student motivation', in D. McInerney and S. Van Etten (eds), *Big Theories Revisited, Vol. 4*, Greenwich, CT: Information Age.

Medway, P. (1996a) 'Constructing the virtual building', in J. Maybin and N. Mercer (eds) *Using English: from conversation to canon*, London: Routledge, with The Open University.

Medway, P. (1996b) 'Virtual and material buildings: construction and constructivism in architecture and writing', *Written Communication*, 13 (4): 473– 514.

Medway P. (1996c) 'Cool people and professional discourse: linguistic "resistance" in the talk of young male architects', *Taboo: the journal of culture and education*, 2 (2): 1–10.

Mercer, A. (2012) *'How Divinely Sweet a Task It Is to Imitate Each Other's Excellencies': Percy Bysshe Shelley, Mary Shelley and the collaborative literary relationship*, M.Phil Dissertation, University of Cambridge.

Mercer, N. (1995) *The Guided Construction of Knowledge: talk amongst teachers and learners*, Clevedon: Multilingual Matters.

Mercer, N. (2000) *Words and Minds: how we use language to think together*, London: Routledge.

Mercer, N. (2004) 'Sociocultural discourse analysis: analysing classroom talk as a social mode of thinking', *Journal of Applied Linguistics*, 1 (2): 137–168.

Mercer, N. (2008) 'The seeds of time: why classroom dialogue needs a temporal analysis', *Journal of the Learning Sciences*, 17 (1): 33–59.

Mercer, N. (in press) 'How might dialogue assist the development of metacognition and self-regulation in the classroom?', *British Journal of Educational Psychology*.

Mercer, N. (2013) 'The social brain, language and goal-directed collective thinking: a social conception of cognition and its implications for understanding how we think, teach and learn', *Educational Psychologist*, 3: 1–21.

Mercer, N. and Hodgkinson, S. (eds) (2008) *Exploring Talk in School*, London: Sage.

Mercer, N. and Littleton, K. (2007) *Dialogue and the Development of Children's Thinking: a sociocultural approach*, London: Routledge.

Mercer, N., Littleton, K. and Wegerif, R. (2004) 'Methods for studying the processes of interaction and collaborative activity in computer-based educational activities', *Technology, Pedagogy and Education*, 13 (2): 193–209.

Mercer, N., Kershner, R., Warwick, P. and Kleine Staarman, J. (2010) 'Can the interactive whiteboard help to provide a 'dialogic space' for children's collaborative activity?', *Language and Education*, 24 (5): 367–384.

Mercier, H. and Sperber, D. (2011) 'Why do humans reason? Arguments for an argumentative theory', *Behavioral and Brain Sciences*, 34 (2): 57–74.

Mesmer-Magnus, J. and DeChurch, L. (2009) 'Information sharing and team performance: a meta-analysis', *Journal of Applied Psychology*, 94 (2): 535–546.

Middleton, D. and Edwards, D. (1990) 'Conversational remembering: a social psychological approach', in D. Middleton and D. Edwards (eds), *Collective Remembering*, London: Sage.

Middup, C., Coughlan, T. and Johnson, P. (2010) 'How creative groups structure tasks through negotiating resources', in M. Lewkowicz, P. Hassanaly, M. Rohde and V. Wulf (eds), *Proceedings of COOP 2010, Computer Supported Cooperative Work*, London: Springer-Verlag.

Miell, D. and Littleton, K. (2008) 'Musical collaboration outside school: processes of negotiation in band rehearsals', *International Journal of Educational Research*, 47 (1): 41–49.

Miller, R. (2011) *Vygotsky in Perspective*, Cambridge: Cambridge University Press.

Moran, S. (2010) 'Creativity in school', in K. Littleton, C. Wood and J. Kleine Staarman (eds), *International Handbook of Psychology in Education*, Bingley: Emerald.

Moran, S. and John-Steiner, V. (2004) 'How collaboration in creative work impacts identity and motivation', in D. Miell and K. Littleton (eds), *Collaborative Creativity: contemporary perspectives*, London: Free Association Books.

Morris, D. and Naughton, J. (1999) 'The future's digital, isn't it? Some experience and forecasts based on the Open University's technology foundation course', *Systems Research and Behavioural Science*, 1 (2): 147–155.

Mukamel R., Ekstrom A., Kaplan J., Iacoboni, M. and Fried, I. (2010) 'Single-neuron responses in humans during execution and observation of actions', *Current Biology*, 20 (8): 750–756.

Muller-Mirza, N. and Perret-Clermont, A.N. (2009) 'Introduction', in N. Muller-Mirza and A.N. Perret-Clermont (eds), *Argumentation and Education: theoretical foundations and practices*, London: Springer.

Nemeth, C. (1995) 'Dissent as driving cognition, attitudes and judgments', *Social Cognition*, 13: 273–291.

Nemeth, C. and Kwan, J. (1985) 'Originality of word associations as a function of majority vs. minority influence', *Social Psychology Quarterly*, 48: 277–282.

Nemeth, C. and Kwan, J. (1987) 'Minority influence, divergent thinking and detection of correct solutions', *Journal of Applied Social Psychology*, 17: 786–797.

Nemeth, C., Rogers, J. and Brown, K. (2001) 'Devil's advocate vs. authentic dissent: stimulating quantity and quality', *European Journal of Social Psychology*, 31 (6): 707–720.

O'Connor, C. and Michaels, S. (1996) 'Shifting participant frameworks: orchestrating thinking practices in group discussion', in D. Hicks (ed.) *Discourse, Learning and Schooling*, Cambridge: Cambridge University Press.

Odean, K. (1990) 'Bear hugs and Bo Dereks on Wall Street', in C. Ricks and L. Michaels (eds), *The State of the Language*, London: Faber and Faber.

Paulus, P.B. and Nijstad, B.A. (2003) *Group Creativity: innovation through collaboration*, New York: University Press.

Paulus, P., Dzindolet, M. and Kohn, N. (2012) 'Collaborative creativity: group creativity and team innovation', in M. Mumford (ed.), *The Handbook of Organizational Creativity*, London: Academic Press.

Peterson, R., Owens, P., Tetlock, K., Fan, E. and Martorana, P. (1998) 'Group dynamics in top management teams: groupthink, vigilance, and alternative models of organizational failure and success', *Organizational Behavior and Management Decision Processes*, 73 (2/3): 272–305.

Pinker, S. (1994) *The Language Instinct*, London: Penguin.

Pinker, S. (2007) *The Stuff of Thought: language as a window into human nature*, London: Penguin.

Premack, D. and Woodruff, G. (1978) 'Does the chimpanzee have a theory of mind?', *Behavioral and Brain Sciences*, 1 (4): 515–526.

Raven, J., Court, J. and Raven, J.C. (1995) *Manual for Raven's Progressive Matrices and Vocabulary Scales*, Oxford: Oxford Psychologists Press.

Reese, E., Haden, C.A. and Fivush, R. (1993) 'Mother–child conversations about the past: relationships of style and memory over time', *Cognitive Development*, 8: 403–430.

Resnick, L.B. (1999) 'Making America smarter', *Education Week Century Series*, 18 (40): 38–40.

Reznitskaya, A., Anderson, R., McNurlen, B., Nguyen-Jahiel, K., Archodidou, A. and Kim, S. (2006) 'Influence of oral discussion on written argument', *Discourse Processes*, 32 (2/3): 155–175.

Rojas-Drummond, S., Albarrán, D. and Littleton, K. (2008) 'Collaboration, creativity and the co-construction of oral and written texts', *Thinking Skills and Creativity*, 3 (3): 177–191.

Rojas-Drummond, S., Littleton, K., Hernandez, F. and Zúñiga, M. (2010) 'Dialogical interactions among peers in collaborative writing contexts', in K. Littleton and C. Howe (eds), *Educational Dialogue: understanding and promoting productive interaction*, London: Routledge.

Rojas-Drummond, S., Mason, N., Littleton, K. and Velez, M. (2012) 'Developing reading comprehension through collaborative learning', *Journal of Research in Reading*, DOI: 10.1111/j.1467-9817.2011.01526.x

Rojas-Drummond, S., Pérez, V., Vélez, M., Gómez, L. and Mendoza, A. (2003) 'Talking for reasoning among Mexican primary school children', *Learning and Instruction*, 13: 653–670.

Runco, M. A. (1999) 'A longitudinal study of exceptional giftedness and creativity', *Creativity Research Journal*, 12 (2): 161–164.

Sawyer, K. (2006) *Explaining Creativity: the science of human innovation*, Oxford: Oxford University Press.

Sawyer, K. (2012) *Explaining Creativity: the science of human innovation (2nd edn)*, Oxford: Oxford University Press.

Sawyer, K. and DeZutter, S. (2009) 'Distributed creativity: how collective creations emerge from collaboration,' *Psychology of Aesthetics, Creativity and the Arts*, 3 (2): 81–92.

Schegloff, E. (1997) 'Whose text? Whose context?', *Discourse and Society*, 8 (2): 165–187.

Schulz-Hardt, S., Brodbeck, F.C., Mojzisch, A., Kerschreiter, R. and Frey, D. (2006) 'Group decision making in hidden profile situations: dissent as a facilitator for decision quality', *Journal of Personality and Social Psychology*, 91: 1080–1093.

Seddon, F. (2004) 'Empathetic creativity: the product of empathetic attunement,' in D. Miell and K. Littleton (eds), *Collaborative Creativity: contemporary perspectives*, London: Free Association Books.

Seddon, F. (2005) 'Modes of communicating during jazz improvising', *British Journal of Music Education*, 22 (1): 47–61.

Sidnell, J. and Stivers, T. (eds) (2012) *Handbook of Conversation Analysis*, Boston, MA: Wiley-Blackwell.

Slavin, R. (2009) 'Cooperative learning', in G. McCulloch and D. Crook (eds), *International Encyclopedia of Education*, Abingdon, UK: Routledge.

Soong, B. and Mercer, N. (2011) 'Improving students' revision of physics concepts through ICT-based co-construction and prescriptive tutoring', *International Journal of Science Education*, 33 (8): 1055–1078.

Soong, B., Mercer, N. and Siew, S.E. (2010) 'Revision by means of computer-mediated peer discussions', *Physics Education*, 45 (3): 264–269.

Stahl, G. (2011) 'Collaborating around the tabletop', *International Journal of Computer-Supported Collaborative Learning*, 6 (4): 485–490.

Stillinger, J. (1991) *Multiple Authorship and the Myth of Solitary Genius*, Oxford: Oxford University Press.

Stone, M. and Thompson, J. (eds) (2006) *Literary Couplings*, Madison, WI: The University of Wisconsin Press.

Storey, H. and Joubert, M.M. (2004) 'The emotional dance of creative collaboration', in D. Miell and K. Littleton (eds), *Collaborative Creativity: contemporary perspectives*, London: Free Association Books.

Surowiecki, J. (2004) *The Wisdom of Crowds*, London: Abacus.

Swales, A. (1990) *Genre Analysis: English in academic and research settings*, Cambridge: Cambridge University Press.

Tolmie, A. and Boyle, J. (2000) 'Factors influencing the success of computer mediated communication (CMC) environments in university teaching: a review and case study', *Computers and Education*, 34 (2): 119–140.

Tomasello, M. (2009) *Why We Cooperate*, Boston, MA: MIT Press.

Torrance, E. P. (1987) *The Torrance Tests of Creative Thinking*, Bensenville, IL: Scholastic Testing Press (Original work published 1974).

Twiner, A. (2011) *Sociocultural Understandings of Technology-Mediated Educational Practices: improvable objects and meaning-making trajectories in the ICT-literate classroom*, Unpublished PhD thesis, The Open University. [Downloadable from: http://oro.open.ac.uk/19908]. Accessed January 22 2013.

Twiner, A., Littleton, K. Coffin, C. and Whitelock, D. (in press) 'Meaning making as an interactional accomplishment: a temporal analysis of intentionality and improvisation in classroom dialogue', *International Journal of Educational Research*.

Underwood, G. and Underwood, J. (1999) 'Task effects on co-operative and collaborative learning with computers', in K. Littleton and P. Light (eds), *Learning with Computers: analysing productive interaction*, London: Routledge.

van Oers, B., Elbers, E., van der Veer, R. and Wardekker, W. (eds) (2008) *The Transformation of Learning: advances in cultural-historical activity theory*, Cambridge: Cambridge University Press.

Vass, E. and Littleton, K. (2010) 'Peer collaboration and learning in the classroom', in K. Littleton, C. Wood and J. Kleine Staarman (eds), *International Handbook of Psychology in Education*, Bingley: Emerald.

Vass, E., Littleton, K., Miell, D. and Jones, A. (2008) 'The discourse of collaborative creative writing: peer collaboration as a context for mutual inspiration', *Thinking Skills and Creativity*, 3 (3): 192–202.

Vauras, M., Iiskala, T., Kajamies, A., Kinnunen, R. and Lehtinen, E. (2003) 'Shared-regulation and motivation of collaborating peers: a case analysis', *Psychologia: an international journal of psychology in the Orient*, 46 (1): 19–37.

Veenman, M. and Spaans, M. (2005) 'Relation between intellectual and metacognitiveskills: age and task difference', *Learning and Individual Differences*, 15: 159–176.

Volet, S.E., Summers, M. and Thurman, J. (2009) 'High-level co-regulation in collaborative learning: how does it emerge and how is it sustained?', *Learning and Instruction*, 19 (2): 128–143.

Vygotsky, L.S. (1962) *Thought and Language*, Cambridge, MA: MIT Press.

Vygotsky, L.S. (1978) *Mind in Society*, Cambridge MA: Harvard University Press.

Warwick, P., Mercer, N. and Kershner, R. (2013) '"Wait, let's just think about this": using the interactive whiteboard and talk rules to scaffold learning for co-regulation in collaborative science activities', *Learning, Culture and Social Interaction*, 2(1): 42–51.

Webb, N.M. (2009) 'The teacher's role in promoting collaborative dialogue in the classroom', *British Journal of Educational Psychology*, 79 (1): 1–28.

Webb, N. and Mastergeorge, A. (2003) 'Promoting effective helping behavior in peer directed groups', *International Journal of Educational Research*, 39 (1–2): 73–97.

Webb, N.M., Nemer, K.M. and Ing, M. (2006) 'Small-group reflections: Parallels between teacher discourse and student behaviour in peer-directed groups', *Journal of the Learning Sciences*, 15 (1): 63–119.

Wegerif, R. (1998) 'The social dimension of asynchronous learning networks', *Journal of Asynchronous Learning Networks*, 2. [Available online at: http://www.aln. org/alnweb/journal/vol2_issue1/Wegerif.pdf]. Accessed 25 July 2003.

Wegerif, R. (2007) *Dialogic, Education and Technology: expanding the space of learning*, London: Springer Verlag.

Wegerif, R. (2010) 'Dialogue and teaching thinking with technology: opening, deepening and expanding the interface', in C. Howe and K. Littleton (eds), *Educational Dialogues: understanding and promoting productive interaction*, London: Routledge.

Wegerif, R. and Dawes (2005) *Thinking and Learning with ICT*, London: RoutledgeFalmer.

Wegerif, R. and Mercer, N. (1997) 'Using computer-based text analysis to integrate quantitative and qualitative methods in the investigation of collaborative learning', *Language and Education*, 11 (4): 271–86.

Wegerif, R. and Scrimshaw, P. (1997) *Computers and Talk in the Primary Classroom,* Clevedon: Multilingual Matters.

Wegerif, R., Perez, J., Rojas-Drummond, S., Mercer, N. and Velez, M. (2005) 'Thinking Together in the UK and Mexico: transfer of an educational innovation', *Journal of Classroom Interaction,* 40 (1): 40–48.

Wells, G. (1999) *Dialogic Enquiry: towards a sociocultural practice and theory of education,* Cambridge: Cambridge University Press.

Wells, G. (2009) *The Meaning Makers: learning to talk and talking to learn (2nd edn),* Bristol: Multilingual Matters.

Wertsch, J.V. (1979) 'From social interaction to higher psychological processes: a clarification and application of Vygotsky's theory', *Human Development,* 51 (1): 66–79.

Wertsch, J. V. (1985) 'Adult–child interaction as a source of self-regulation in children', in S. R. Yussen (ed.), *The Growth of Reflection in Children,* Orlando, FL: Academic Press.

Whitebread, D. and Pino Pasternak, D. (2010) 'Metacognition, self-regulation and meta-knowing', in K. Littleton, C. Wood and J. Kleine Staarman (eds), *International Handbook of Psychology in Education,* Bingley: Emerald.

Whyte, W.H. (1952) 'Groupthink', *Fortune,* March Issue.

Wilson, E.O. (2012) *The Social Conquest of Earth,* New York: Liveright Publishing/ W. W. Norton and Company.

Winne, P. and Hadwin, A. (2008) 'The weave of motivation and self-regulated learning', in D. Schunk and B. Zimmerman (eds), *Motivation and Self-Regulated Learning: theory, research and applications,* New York: Taylor & Francis.

Wolf, M., Crosson, A. and Resnick, L. (2006) 'Accountable talk in reading comprehension instruction', *CSE Technical Report 670,* Learning and Research Development Center, Pittsburgh, PA: University of Pittsburgh.

Woolley, A., Chabris, C., Pentland, A., Hashmi, N. and Malone, T. (2010) 'Evidence for a collective intelligence factor in the performance of human groups', *Science,* 330 (6004): 686–688.

Yoshida, M. (2002) *Lesson Study: an introduction,* Madison, NJ: Global Educational Resources.

Young, S. (2008) 'Collaboration between 3- and 4-year-olds in self-initiated play on instruments', *International Journal of Educational Research,* 47 (1): 3–10.

Zimmerman, B.J. (2008) 'Investigating self-regulation and motivation: historical background, methodological developments, and future prospects', *American Educational Research Journal,* 45 (1): 166–183.

INDEX

Note: Page numbers in *italics* are for tables, those in **bold** are for figures.